Roch

Keith Fennell was born in 1973. At the age of 21 he joined the elite Australian Special Air Service Regiment. He was deployed on many operations, including missions to Afghanistan, East Timor, the Solomon Islands and the southern Indian Ocean. Fennell also served on a medical deployment to East Africa, was a member of the boarding party in the controversial MV *Tampa* incident, and supported counter-terrorist operations for the 2002 Commonwealth Heads of Government Meeting in Brisbane and the Sydney 2000 Olympic Games.

Fennell left the SAS in late 2002 and moved to the United Arab Emirates, where he was employed as a special operations adviser. In January 2004, Fennell accepted a position in Iraq, and he spent the next 30 months running operations there, in Afghanistan and in Banda Aceh. In June 2006 Fennell returned to Australia. He published his first book, *Warrior Brothers*, in 2008 and it quickly became a best-seller. He is now completing a double-degree in Creative Arts and Arts at the University of Wollongong. Fennell lives with his wife and three children on the South Coast of New South Wales.

By the same author

Warrior Brothers: My Life in the Australian SAS

WARRIOR TRAINING

KEITH FENNELL

BANTAM
SYDNEY AUCKLAND TORONTO NEW YORK LONDON

Note to readers: Underwater training can be extremely dangerous and should only be performed under competent and close supervision.

A Bantam book
Published by Random House Australia Pty Ltd
Level 3, 100 Pacific Highway, North Sydney NSW 2060
www.randomhouse.com.au

First published by Bantam in 2009
This edition published by Bantam in 2010

Addresses for companies within the Random House Group can be found at
www.randomhouse.com.au/offices

National Library of Australia
Cataloguing-in-Publication Entry

Fennell, Keith.
Warrior training.

ISBN 978 1 74275 014 9 (pbk).

Fennell, Keith – Biography.
Australia. Army. Special Air Service Regiment – Biography.
Soldiers – Australia – Biography.
Soldiers – Training of – Australia.
Combat – Physiological aspects.

355.50994

Photograph on page 198 courtesy of Stephen Chu
Cover photographs courtesy of Keith Fennell and SuperStock
Cover design by blacksheep-uk.com
Internal design and typesetting by Midland Typesetters, Australia
Printed in Australia by Griffin Press, an accredited ISO AS/NZS 14001:2004 Environmental Management System printer

10 9 8 7 6 5 4 3 2 1

MIX
Paper from
responsible sources
FSC® C009448

The paper this book is printed on is certified against the Forest Stewardship Council® Standards. Griffin Press holds FSC chain of custody certification SGS-COC-005088. FSC promotes environmentally responsible, socially beneficial and economically viable management of the world's forests.

CONTENTS

For my grandparents, Gerard and Mary.

And my parents, Bob and Shirley.

PROLOGUE

Not all SAS soldiers enjoy parachuting. While jammed in the back of a 22-seater bus on our way to RAAF Base Pearce for jump training, I noticed that one of the guys was white-faced, his hands gripping the seat in front of him in the same way that children sink their fingers into their parents' arms while on a rollercoaster for the first time. He looked like he was about to vomit.

'Hey, mate,' I said. 'You feeling crook?'

'I hate this shit,' he answered, relaxing his grip and pushing his head into the seat.

'What, driving to Pearce?'

He laughed. 'Nah, parachuting, smartarse. This shit freaks me out.'

I sat confused for a moment, trying to comprehend why someone who hated parachuting would put himself through the rigours of life as an SAS soldier. 'What about abseiling, climbing, diving – do you get off on any of them?'

'Get off?' he said. 'Definitely not. I get off on sex.'

'Fair enough – but then why are you in the Regiment?'

All SAS soldiers must overcome their fears.

'Because I wanted to test myself, to prove I could cut it.'

This guy – a quiet, unassuming man – was a solid performer. He went on to scare the shit out of himself for another six years before deciding enough was enough. It requires a strong mind to continually embrace fear rather than run the other way. In my view, the toughest men in the Regiment weren't those who enjoyed what was thrown their way, but those who were uncomfortable and yet managed to keep their fears in check.

In battle soldiers will experience a range of feelings, from fear to exhilaration, depending on the intensity of the engagement. So what separates the men who hold their nerve from those who don't? I believe that training and mental preparation are vital to performing well under adverse conditions. When things go wrong, you cannot simply succumb to your natural survival instincts; you have to make decisions based on sound judgement.

My aim in this book is to inspire readers to believe in themselves and to reflect upon how they deal with adversity. Regardless of whether you're a doctor in Afghanistan, a student in Great Britain, a miner in Australia or a tour guide in Tanzania, self-belief and thorough preparation are critical to success.

By the time most people reach old age – if they manage to hang around that long – they will have experienced the best and worst of life, from love and the thrill of achieving their dreams, to failure, heartache and death. They are wise, for they have lived.

Many soldiers also gain a wide range of experiences, from forging life-long friendships and overcoming exciting and challenging tasks, to dealing with immense hardship and staring down death. This is particularly so for special-forces soldiers due to the rigor of their training and operational deployments. But rather than absorbing these golden highs and brutal lows over an entire lifetime, a soldier might experience them in a few weeks, months or years.

Men and women often return from war different people. Some struggle with what they have seen, while others are able to rationalise their experiences, contextualise events and use the lessons they have learnt to propel them through life. Many SAS soldiers fall into this latter category, which is a tribute to their self-belief, determination and mental strength, and to the incredible training they receive. But what happens to these soldiers when they leave the Regiment? This book offers an insight into the training and mindset of SAS soldiers, and how we negotiate the transition between two vastly different lives.

=

Ever since I was young, I have been intrigued by high-performing individuals and teams, especially those who excel in challenging or adverse conditions. How do they do it? What makes them tick?

Since the formation of the Australian Special Air Service Regiment in 1957, fewer than 1500 soldiers have earned the right to wear the highly coveted 'sandy beret'. Even during difficult times – after the devastating loss of 15 SAS soldiers in Townsville in 1996, for example, when two Blackhawk helicopters collided during counter-terrorism training – the Regiment won't lower its impeccable standards just to fill positions. Only those who show potential and pass the rigorous selection process are accepted.

SAS soldiers must not only display exceptional levels of physical fitness and endurance, they must also be team-oriented, able to think clearly during high-stress situations, and capable of processing a large amount of information in a relatively short period of time. Applicants don't have to be Olympic athletes and brain surgeons, but they must possess a particular mindset that enables them to prepare themselves physically and mentally for the challenges they will endure on SAS operational deployments. I love this about the Regiment – irrespective of how thin the ranks become, its standards never waver.

It wasn't until I left the SAS in December 2002 and spent several years as a private contractor running operations in Iraq and Afghanistan that I truly appreciated the extraordinary quality of the men who make it into the SAS. The Regiment, like any organisation, has an internal pecking order. Soldiers are continuously assessed, rated and counselled by their superiors; this guarantees that each soldier is aware of his own strengths and weaknesses. The men are also assessed informally by their peers. Due to the challenging nature of SAS training and operations, every man becomes highly conscious of his own ability, and of the ability of the men around him. There is nowhere to hide.

Every SAS squadron has its 'jets' (those who are a cut above), its 'average Joes' (the majority), and its poorer performers (those who hover around the minimum standard required). But after 30 months contracting in Iraq and Afghanistan, where I attempted to mould a contingent of men from contrasting military backgrounds and nationalities into a formidable security force, I realised that *all* SAS soldiers – even those who are performing at the lower end of their experience levels – are exceptional.

=

Following the publication of *Warrior Brothers* in 2008, I received many messages of support from former and current soldiers, and from non-military people, including one email from a man who had been contemplating suicide. He was inspired by the actions of some of my friends and changed his mind. I received another note from an 83-year-old woman who had lived through decades of angst after her husband had returned from World War II a different man. He has since passed away, but she found something in *Warrior Brothers* that gave her a sense of why he was the way he was.

I never expected an elderly woman – besides my Nan – to read my book, let alone to take the time to drop me a line. Her letter moved me but, to be honest, it was not for that reason that I'd written *Warrior Brothers*. For me, writing was cathartic; it allowed me to document my thoughts and to interrogate my inner self. Initially, I had no intention of letting others read the material; I just wanted to get it out of my system. In some respects, my computer's hard drive had a more honest account of who I was than most of my family and friends did.

As my email inbox began to swell with hundreds of messages, I was humbled – blown away, really – that others were drawing strength and inspiration from some of the people and experiences I had written about. I hope this book offers more of the same.

1

CRAVING A CHANGE OF LIFE

As a young man growing up I had no idea that Australia had a special-forces unit called the Special Air Service Regiment. Then I read an article about an SAS team being involved in an incident in Somalia, which gave a vague description of what the SAS was and what its soldiers did. If I was to pinpoint the exact moment that I decided to strive for the SAS, then that would be it. The actions of the hard-hitting guys at the centre of that incident inspired me.

I had been restless for a couple of years. I was 19, and although I had contemplated leaving my trade as a motor mechanic before I was fully qualified, my father had encouraged me to persevere.

'Look, mate,' he'd said, 'I know you want a job that's exciting, but if you hang around for two years and

At 17, my job as an apprentice motor mechanic didn't do it for me.

get your ticket, then I'm sure you'll get your chance.'

He was right. Sitting in the military recruitment office and watching a video of soldiers parachuting was all the motivation I needed to join the army.

When I met the recruiting officer, I did my best to act cool and not sound desperate. But I couldn't help asking: 'If I join the army, do I get to parachute?'

'Providing you meet the medical and physical requirements, there's a very good chance,' he replied, as a slight, sardonic smirk worked its way to the corner of his mouth.

I tried not to grin, thinking I had just nailed the scam of the century. *Who gets paid to jump out of planes?*

The recruiting officer had a cloth parachute badge on his right shoulder, the mark of one who was qualified. I bet that he, too, was trying to remain straight-faced: he knew very well that real military parachuting was vastly different from the recruiting videos he had just shown me. The videos were filled with images of soldiers jumping out the back of planes and gliding through the sky under canopy. But they never showed footage of anyone landing.

I asked the recruiting officer another question: 'Are there decent gyms in the army?'

He smiled the sort of smile that said: *You fuckwit — of course there are decent gyms in the army.* But his answer was a little more diplomatic. 'The army has some of the best training establishments in the country.'

So I get to parachute and train in the gym, I thought. *Where do I sign up?*

I filled out the appropriate paperwork, enrolled at TAFE to further my education, and waited. I must have called the recruiting office half a dozen times to check on my application. And then it came – an official-looking letter announcing my test dates.

So in October 1993 I travelled to Sydney for my medical, psychological and aptitude testing. If I was found suitable then I would be interviewed later that afternoon. I passed the initial tests with no problems. One of the first questions I was asked during my interview was: 'If you were sent to war, could you kill a person?'

I was so pumped to have made the interview stage that I'm surprised I didn't say something like: 'If you let me in the army then I'm happy to kill as many people as you want.' But in reality my thoughts then were much the same as they are now. 'It would not be something that I would enjoy,' I said, 'but if I was confronted by a situation where I was required to take a life in order to save mine or another, then I would.'

Saying goodbye to my parents. I joined the army at the age of 20.

My application was approved, and a few months later – on 25 January 1994 – I joined the Australian Army.

≡

Our induction ceremony was held in Sydney before we were herded onto buses and driven to 1RTB – the 1st Recruit Training Battalion at Kapooka, Wagga Wagga. During the ceremony one enthusiastic guy told me that he had been in the Army Reserve, and that I should let him know if I needed a hand. Apparently polishing boots and brass was 'a piece of piss'. Within three days of our arrival at Kapooka, this same guy walked into my room and said: 'Fennell, you have to help me escape! I can't take this shit anymore. I gotta get out of here – I'm goin' crazy!'

He was an intense little bastard with a red face and wiry physique, but he was also a little crazy – in a likeable and humorous way. The next night – wearing just a pair of grandpa-type underpants – he came into my room asking for change so he could grab a Coke from the machine downstairs. Lights out was at 2200 hours; anyone caught out of bed after this time was going to have their face yelled off and possibly be subjected to some bullshit punishment like scrubbing bathroom tiles with a tooth-brush. Besides that, the Coke machine was at the bottom of 'God's stairs', an internal stairwell that was only to be used by our instructors.

I couldn't fathom why anyone would want to run the gauntlet for a can of Coke, but I got out of bed, unlocked my cupboard and pulled a two-dollar coin out of my wallet.

'Thanks, man – I owe you one,' he said as he scurried down the hall.

The next thing I heard was his can of Coke slamming into the bottom tray of the machine. Anyone within 100 metres would have heard it. *Surely he'll get busted on the way back to his room*, I laughed to myself. A minute later he strolled into my room with a large smile on his face, drawing on his can of Coke like he was a gangster suck-ing on a Cuban.

'Hey, Fennell, want a sip?'

I visualised his sweaty lips on the can, held back a dry-retch and refused the offer. 'No thanks, mate. You have it.'

'I'll put the change in your drawer.'

'Cool.'

Within five seconds of him leaving my room and re-entering his own, which was just across the hallway, an angry white light burst through the doorway.

'Which one of you fucks was out of bed?'

Neither I nor my room-mate answered.

The angry prick – the duty corporal – turned on the light. 'Were you out of bed?'

'No, sir,' I replied.

'I'm a corporal, fuckwit.' He turned on my room-mate: 'Was it you?'

'No, Corporal.'

'I saw someone's shadow near the window. Who was it?'

I opted to play dumb. 'I don't know, Corporal.'

The duty corporal was aware that unless we admitted it, there wasn't a lot he could do. He turned off the light, shone his torch into the room opposite, then disappeared down the hallway.

The next morning, during a routine inspection while we were having breakfast, our section commander found the loose change in my drawer. I was yelled at for nearly 10 minutes and accused of promoting thievery. When quizzed as to how the money got there, I said I planned to use it for the pay phone when we were allowed to call home.

'Call home? I'll tell you when you can call home, fuck-wit. Do you understand?'

'Yes, Corporal.'

'Next time you'll be charged with insecurity. Get out of my sight, shit-stain.'

I marched up the hallway and straight into the room of the guy who put the change in my drawer.

'Hey, Fennell, what'd he say?'

'He asked me why the money was in my drawer and I told them you put it there. You have to go to the office.'

'Man, you're shittin' me?'

'Yeah, I am.' I left his room laughing.

The only things I enjoyed about basic training were the physical training, our four-day furlough and the couple of nights we had on the piss. Getting yelled at didn't really do it for me, but some of the one-liners were amusing. While marching back from the range, my section commander yelled: 'Hey, Barrington, close your fucking hand when you march or I'll come over there and stick my dick in it!' Even in the Regiment, soldiers on selection are sometimes surprised by the odd witty remark. On one course, the trainees were lined up waiting for their turn in the shower when one of the senior instructors – a guy with an ability to remain completely deadpan – bellowed: 'Trainee 66, you've got a great arse. What do you feed that thing – cock?'

I can honestly say that I entered the army with one aim in mind: to join the SAS as quickly as possible. The physical training we did at Kapooka was only mildly challenging, as most of the pack marches and runs had to allow for the soldiers at the bottom of the group. We were constantly reminded that the army was about teamwork – a section is only as fast as its slowest man.

Negotiating obstacles during basic training.

At times I found this frustrating, as the physical standard of some guys was so far below what I expected that it was painful. When someone puts in, regardless of what level they are at, then no probs. But when someone dives on the ground like they've just been shot after a casual 500-metre run, then I tend to question their commitment to the team. I longed to be part of a hard-hitting group of men who all wanted to go the extra mile. I'd seen *Chariots of Fire*. If we had to run, then that's how I wanted it to be.

At Kapooka I met a few like-minded people, so each evening we would supplement our training with sets of chin-ups, push-ups and sit-ups. As for our section commanders giving us grief, well, there appeared to be some sort of code – they left us alone while we were training. During one of our evening sessions, one man, Dalton – a blond-haired guy with a sharp sense of humour – passed a comment that gave me confidence.

'Hey, Fennell, I reckon you're going to make it into the SAS.'

I finished the push-ups I was doing, then faced him and raised an eyebrow, thinking he was taking the piss.

'I'm serious . . . you're focused, man. There has to be guys who get in, and I think you'll be one of 'em.'

≡

Our platoon was expected to be sent to the infantry training centre in Singleton, but as it was already at full capacity we were sent straight to Brisbane, along with another nine or 10 platoons – some 300 soldiers in all. Although the training program there was comparable, I did feel a little ripped-off. We arrived at Enoggera, in Brisbane, in the early afternoon; unlike at Kapooka, where we'd been met by half a dozen screaming instructors, our opening address was almost civil. Later that day we were taken for a run around the area and introduced to Enoggera Hill. The weather was humid, the road steep. I have no doubt that Townsville's Castle Hill and Enoggera Hill in Brisbane are two of the most challenging short runs around.

Over the next three months we were trained as infanteers. The physical training (PT) – a blend of circuits, runs

Obstacle course, basic training.

and battle training – was brilliant. My favourite session was the obstacle course: a series of walls, river crossings, traverse ropes and towers. Towards the end of our infantry training, Rog – a stocky and confident soldier – and I applied for the SAS selection course. We both passed the physical, aptitude and psychological testing and were fortunate to be given the chance to attempt the course the following year. Most infantry soldiers are required to spend a couple of years in the Battalion.

We had no idea what we were in for – the challenge was daunting. If we were to listen to all the negative comments about how impossible it was to make it into the SAS, then we would have failed the course before it even began. At the completion of infantry training, I was presented with an award for 'best at physical training', which definitely enhanced my confidence.

I tried to imagine what sort of man made it into the SAS. How much fitter or stronger could they be? Physically,

Rog and I were in the best shape of our lives. We just had to believe in ourselves. I had never met an SAS soldier or knew anyone who had passed the selection course, but I was certain that even SAS soldiers were human.

Our platoon spent most of the next five months on field training exercises near Quilpe, a hot, dry area 1000 kilometres west of Brisbane. One late afternoon our section was allocated a defensive position along the bank of a river. I was lying near a log and kept myself amused by taking aim at a couple of sheep that were grazing on the opposite bank. There didn't appear to be a lot to eat.

I had a sick sense that someone or something was looking at me. My right ribs were flush against a large hole in the log. I shuffled back a little and peered inside. I was initially intrigued by a pair of beady dark eyes less than 20 centimetres from mine. I thought they belonged to a mouse. Then the creature stuck out its tongue and slithered towards me.

Instantly I lost all composure. 'Aahh!' I shouted as I rolled out of the way, my left hand coming up to protect my neck. The snake followed me, positioned itself atop the log and flared its neck. It was a healthy specimen with a girth the size of my lower arm.

Locky, a bushy who was a natural with a rifle, also leapt out of the way. 'Hey, Keithy, when you get back to Brisbane go and get yourself a lottery ticket. That's a king brown. If it had nailed ya' on the face or neck out here then it would have been all over.'

I didn't say anything but just stood there holding my neck.

Locky looked at my face and laughed.

'I thought it was a mouse so I didn't bother moving,' I said.

'You fuckin' idiot,' said Locky, laughing harder.

≡

In October 1994 our platoon was sent to Brunei for a month of jungle training. Vietnam movies like *Platoon* give an accurate impression of the sounds, insects and weather of jungle operations, but I was still surprised, after just a five-day patrol, by how taxing that environment can be.

The humidity underneath the canopy is stifling. With no breeze, the air remains thick and dense. I have seen guys hyperventilate and panic during arduous physical activity. They complain of not being able to breathe; they gasp, with large frightened eyes, like a smoker who suffers from emphysema. Everyone is soaked from head to toe by his own perspiration. If a patrol is to last for five days, then you generally remain wet for five days.

Jungle training camp, Brunei.

When your skin stays wet in a humid environment, the onset of 'prickly heat' or heat rash is inevitable. The pores of your skin become clogged, meaning the skin struggles to breathe. As the sweat glands release fluid, the moisture is trapped beneath the skin, creating a profound stinging sensation and a red rash.

The first time I experienced prickly heat was while eating a canteen of steaming noodles in the Bruneian jungle. I was nearing the end of my meal when, as a result of the hot food inside my stomach, I began to sweat. I stopped eating – which in itself is significant! – and pulled up my shirt, as I was certain I was being mauled by insects. After one of the boys checked my back and gave me the all clear, I resumed eating. As the hot noodles slid down my oesophagus into my stomach, my body began to perspire again.

What in the hell is going on? I thought. I felt as though my skin was bursting underneath the surface. Upon further inspection, a mate noticed I had a red rash all over my ribs and back.

'You've got heat rash,' said another. 'It sucks – I get it all the time.' He then pulled out a couple of alcohol swabs and scrubbed my back. Instant relief!

When operating in the jungle, depending on the tactical situation, you should always attempt to go to bed dry. As a minimum, we learnt to replace our socks or our feet would soon rot. Having said that, soldiers will generally only carry one spare set of clothing, and monsoonal rain is pretty difficult to hide from. Within three days, most of our clothing and sleeping equipment would be damp. Then it's just a matter of sucking it up and enjoying the experience for what it is – a chance to bond with nature.

One time, while lying in an ambush and being belted by rain on a training exercise, the guy to my left side looked at me and smiled.

'That's better,' he whispered.

'Did you just do a piss?' I asked, a disturbed look on my face.

'Yeah, I was freezing. Now I'm warm.'

Some men are able to hold it together and some aren't. While on patrol, our platoon was instructed to halt while the section commanders conferred with the platoon commander. I was the section 2IC and sat on the track with everyone else. My section commander was annoyed with this and thought I should know better. Unable to control his frustration, on his way back through the men he launched a boot into my right kidney. I was caught unaware and winded. My face filled with blood, my eyes flashed. It was a struggle, but I dumped my pack and began to stand up. He had apologised before I was on my feet, so my angry red face and I sat back down.

By December of 1994 I was nearing the end of a promotion course – subject two for corporal – and was looking forward to getting home for a few weeks. In my quest to be different, I left a message on my girlfriend's answering machine. I rambled on with some banal account of what we'd been up to before casually asking her to marry me. I didn't find out her answer for 10 days. My anxious wait ended with the completion of the field phase of the course. Colleen said yes.

Our final parade was held at the 8/9 RAR boozer. I didn't bother having a beer. The remainder of our platoon had been granted leave a week before. Three of us – including Bradd, a mate who would later make it into the Regiment and narrowly avoid being turned into a tea strainer by the Taliban – decided to drive from Brisbane to Sydney as soon as we knocked off. We left in a convoy: three shitty cars with three impatient drivers. We hadn't had a decent night's sleep for nearly 10 days. The sensible thing to have done would have been to tackle the drive the following morning after a full night's sleep. Instead, driven by impatience and a strong desire for sex, we rolled out of Enoggera at 1600 that afternoon.

Nine hours later I woke up to the sound of tyres on gravel and a honking horn. My car had left the road, and I was lucky to avoid some large trees. I had fallen asleep, and chances were it would happen again. Bradd had seen my car drift then leave the road, so he'd slammed his hand on the horn.

I got out of my car and approached the white lights behind me, embarrassed and half-grinning.

'I just saved your life, dickhead,' said Bradd, smiling.

'Yeah, that was close. I'm going to get my head down for a few hours,' I said.

'Yeah, I felt myself go a couple of times too,' said Bradd. 'What time do you wanna get going?'

'About five . . . or whenever we wake up,' I said.

We made it home and I got engaged. For me, life carried on.

=

I enjoyed my time in the Battalion, but I was never content. Training for the SAS selection course dominated my thoughts the way a writer dreams of getting published. My desire to be an SAS soldier was all-consuming.

2

THE SAS: ALL OR NOTHING

There are those in life who whine about missed opportunities. 'I could have made the Olympic swim team . . . I've always wanted to trek through Nepal . . . I could have been a doctor . . . I wish I'd spent more time with my kids when they were young . . . I should have tried out for the SAS . . .'

Some people prefer to pull others down, to make excuses about why others have achieved — rather than addressing the real reasons for why they themselves did not. Surely those who spend hours worrying about what others are doing would be a little more content if they kept life simple and concentrated on themselves. Then there are people who call others lucky: 'She's lucky, he's lucky, they're lucky . . . I'm so unlucky.'

I believe people generally create their own luck — it's called hard work.

While I was training for the SAS selection course, I was chastised by one man who had recently been posted to the 6th Battalion as a section commander. He'd previously been a member of a reconnaissance platoon in one of the

Townsville infantry battalions and had a grandiose opinion of himself. When he heard I was panelled for selection even though I had only been in the army for 10 months, he became irritated.

'Hey, private – I hear you're doing the Cadre Course,' he began.

'Yes,' I said.

'Yes, *Corporal*,' he replied with a sly grin on his face, looking to his left and right to make sure others were taking notice.

I bit my tongue and played the game. 'Yes, Corporal.' There was no doubt about it. *You're a tool*, I thought.

'How much fuckin' nav ya' done?' he asked, referring to navigation.

'I completed subject two for corporal, which enabled me to square my nav away, Corporal.'

'Huh, I heard about that fuckin' course. The Cadre is nearly all nav. It takes a soldier three or four years to get the skills. Without solid nav, you won't have a chance.'

I found out afterwards that this guy had previously attempted selection. He made it to the end of the first week. I made a mental note of our conversation and used it on selection for motivation when things got tough.

=

The army was beginning to look like an all or nothing option, at least in the short term. If I failed the SAS selection course, then I was to be discharged from full time service. I joined the Ready Reserve scheme, a one-year commitment, due to missing the regular enlistment by a few weeks. I was not prepared to wait another 12 months

On exercises in south-east Queensland with the 6th Battalion.

and was told during enlistment that I would be able to transfer to the regular army at the completion of my 12-month obligation. The training was the same so I signed on. What we weren't told was that the politicians were determined to make the scheme a success. For this to happen, soldiers were required to return for 35 days of continuation training each year. Obviously, if soldiers were absorbed into the regular army, this would not be possible. It was decided that soldiers who had completed promotion or specialist courses were of value to the scheme so would not be offered regular positions. You gotta love performance punishment. At the end of the year, seven soldiers from our company were offered the opportunity to join the regular army. My platoon sergeant, Howie, knew I would be pissed so called me into his office.

'Hey, Fennell, the army, just like life, isn't always fair. What can we do about it? Nothin'. You want regs?'

'Yes, Sergeant,' I replied.

'Then all you gotta do is pass the selection course. If you don't get injured you'll go alright. You're fit enough. Don't worry about how long you've been in the army. Those SAS flogbags will teach ya' everything you need to know.'

I liked Howie. Behind his fiery sergeant persona, was a man who cared about his guys.

'I was a sergeant by 26 and now I'm a fat bastard who gets to sort out admin bullshit for guys like you.'

His honesty made me laugh.

'You'd get bored in the battalion. Why stuff around, you know what ya' want. Now piss off and go run up the mountain or do whatever bullshit you need to do to make sure you get in.'

I thanked Howie for his advice and left his office feeling pumped. I was getting married so it would have been nice to have had the security of a fulltime job if I failed the course, but the uncertainty made me more determined.

≡

After our engagement party, Col and I returned to Canberra, where she was employed at a local radio station. While she was at work, I would train, preparing myself for the SAS selection course. After a few days, a couple of mates, Arny and Rog, came down to visit. Rog, who looked a little like Tom Cruise – when Tom Cruise was still cool – was also with us when Col selected her engagement ring. She has never been intimidated by the relationships I have with my mates. In a sense, my brothers are her brothers.

Rog and I were both attempting selection, so we donned packs and tackled some of the mountains around Canberra. I had marvelled at the steepness of the terrain many times and often aspired to take them on. Although the area was private property, I couldn't resist the temptation to scale a steep mountain. For me, walking somewhere for the first time, taking in the angles, colours, vegetation and terrain, is far more exhilarating than a ride on a roller-coaster. I get to choose the speed of ascent and how hard I make my heart beat. It's a time when money and possessions mean nothing, like taking off on a wave, when the immediacy of living the moment means complete and utter freedom.

The immediacy of living the moment.

If I succeeded and was accepted into the SAS, then Col and I would be moving to Perth. In Canberra, Col's boss and close friend Jacqueline was less than thrilled at the prospect of Colleen being taken away. She thought SAS soldiers were psychopaths, so from the day I met her she referred to me as 'Killer'.

'So, Killer, tell me – what are you going to do if you don't make it into the SAS?'

I felt like I was being interrogated by my girlfriend's father. I had no idea what else I wanted to do. My sole employment ambition was to join the SAS. Nothing else turned me on. Being unemployed and clueless about where I was heading was not the answer Colleen's over-protective friend wanted to hear. So I said: 'I'd go to uni and get a degree.'

'Really . . . What will you study?'

God, who is this woman? I thought. 'Mathematics. I'll be a maths teacher,' I said with little conviction. I had as much desire to be a maths teacher as I did to return to my trade as a motor mechanic – none.

'A maths teacher? Where will you live?'

A long way from you. 'Brisbane, perhaps back in Wollongong,' I said, realising the importance of getting Col's friend and boss onside.

'What about Canberra?' she asked.

Not as long as you're still there. 'We haven't discussed where we'd live,' I said.

Colleen wasn't concerned in the slightest and let Jac know that she would definitely be moving to Perth. 'He'll get in,' she said, as she poured chocolate syrup over her favourite meal – pancakes and ice cream.

I appreciated Col's belief in me, but although I knew I would never voluntarily remove myself from the course, I planned to approach the course just one day at a time. Colleen maintained this unflinching confidence in my ability throughout my years in the Regiment, never allowing the thought that I could be killed. This wasn't the case during my time running operations in Iraq and Afghanistan as a contractor, however. Waking up in the middle of the night drenched in perspiration as I wrestled with tactical options did catch her attention when I was at home.

Despite keeping Col well-informed – and this helped – it wasn't until she read *Warrior Brothers* and gained access to some of my most private thoughts that she fully realised the fragility of the soldier's lifestyle.

=

I returned to the Battalion in Brisbane on 4 January 1995. The SAS selection course was 11 weeks away. Three days later we deployed up north for our final six-week training exercise. Although it was difficult to find the time for extra training sessions when we were out bush, Rog and I were issued double rations. Instead of eating one disgusting can of ham and egg each day, we were able to chow down on two. This would have to be my least favourite meal in the military. Purely out of interest, I have eaten dog food before – both the tinned and biscuit varieties. The biscuits are alright, but tinned dog food is very, very average. Still, I would probably consider ham and egg to be even viler.

Due to exercise constraints, we were afforded very little time to train. A couple of 3.2-kilometre webbing runs, augmented with push-up and sit-up circuits, were as good as it got. But that all changed as soon as we returned to Brisbane. Where possible, we followed the SAS's three-month training program, pounding the roads and tracks around Enoggera. But it didn't take long for our feet to fall apart. We tried everything, from wearing a thin second pair of socks, to regular soakings with Condy's crystals and spraying our feet with methylated spirits diluted with water. We'd already missed several weeks of training so, rather than allowing our feet time to heal, we taped them up and kept going.

On one stifling morning Rog and I each loaded two concrete blocks and a 20-litre jerry can into our packs before scrambling up the mountain. I didn't know which part of my body hurt most – my feet, legs, back and shoulders, or my lungs, which were rising and falling at an alarming rate. The only motivation we got was from each other. If I wanted to take my pack off, sit down and take time out, I could. I knew I didn't have to be there and that the pain was self-inflicted, my own doing. In the back of my mind was a niggling little voice, which reminded me that although I was putting in the effort, there was no guarantee I would pass the course. But I decided that if the program said that I was to wear a pack and punish myself for three hours, then that's what I would do.

My preparation for selection wasn't ideal – I suffered damaged ankle ligaments, was on crutches for a while, had infected feet and faced the possibility of a medical discharge. I had a choice. I could look for excuses, justify them to myself and then perhaps try again the following year. (I knew of a sniper from the Battalion who had trained for selection four times, and each time he had pulled out the week before departure. He never did make it onto the course.) Or I could give it a go.

Life very rarely turns out the way we think it should. Those who wait for everything to line up perfectly before tackling their dreams are often the same people who arrive at the penultimate years of their life frustrated about what might have been. I decided that I would never live this way.

So I had a dodgy ankle – big deal. The army had shit-loads of strapping tape.

≡

To pass the SAS selection course, you need to be self-motivated, disciplined and capable of setting mid- to long-term goals, and you have to have an ability to follow through when things become challenging. Those who are successful are not supermen. They just know what they want and are prepared to put in a great deal of effort to make it happen. Anyone who attains the top of their chosen field shares these attributes.

We are all motivated to achieve different things in life. I am drawn to new challenges and excitement. I am competitive by nature, but I don't gauge my success by comparing myself to others. Thinking about what someone else earns, owns, is doing or has done is negative. It makes you dissatisfied, destroys your self-esteem and prevents you from reaching your potential. Irrespective of what others around me are doing, I set my own goals and try to be relentless in my quest to achieve them.

I've also tried never to be discouraged by negative comments; instead, I often use them for motivation. When someone says 'You haven't been in the army long enough to pass the SAS selection course' or 'You should finish your degree before you write a book', they enhance my desire to achieve. The motivation is already there, but I'm constantly searching for ways to make it stronger – whatever it takes to give me the edge I need.

Each year hundreds of applicants apply for the SAS selection course. The screening process, designed to weed out those who are unsuitable, begins nine months before the course. Applicants must pass the special-forces barrier test in order to prove they are physically capable of beginning the training. If a soldier fails to attain the minimum physical requirements, he will not be accepted onto the course because it's unlikely he will be able to complete the arduous three-month training program.

The next test assessed aptitude; it was the same test that applicants complete when they apply for the Australian Defence Force. SAS soldiers must be able to think clearly under stress and be able to absorb information quickly. Soldiers are graded on their ability to answer questions quantitatively and qualitatively. There is also a detailed section on problem-solving. The test isn't designed to be completed – there are too many questions. An applicant either displays the minimum aptitude required or doesn't.

The next test was a 300-question psychological examination. 'When you're standing in a room, do you feel like people are staring at you from dark corners?' Who in his right mind would say yes to that? Rationally, it was relatively easy to work out what you were supposed to answer. There were many questions like this, framed in different ways. The assessors were looking for consistency and I took a reserved approach when answering the questions.

During my interview, I was questioned about one answer I'd given.

'Private Fennell, in your psychological examination you answered that you didn't know if you had a higher tolerance to pain than most other people. Please explain the reasoning behind your answer.'

'From a young age, I have always pushed myself physically,' I said. 'But it's impossible for me to ascertain if my pain threshold is superior to others', as I don't know what other people are feeling. The only serious accident I've had was a broken arm when I was young. I don't recall how I handled that situation.'

'But if we were to ask you whether you thought you could push yourself further than most people, which is something that is required of an SAS soldier, then what would you say?'

I grinned and realised that they were basically telling me the answer they needed to hear.

'From what I have seen when I'm training with my peers in the Battalion,' I said, 'I think I do have an ability to extend myself further than others.'

'Thank you,' the assessor said.

And thank you, I thought.

3

WEEK ONE: EXPOSING WHAT LIES BENEATH

Only those who show potential are accepted into the SAS selection course. The number of applicants varies from year to year. One course might begin with 80 men, another with double this number. On our course there were 150 starters.

The first nine days of selection are designed to shock the participants and wear them down. The soldiers must pass many physical tests. If a soldier fails to make the minimum cut-off time on a run, he might be allowed one re-test. If he fails this, he's generally removed from the course. The first week is also when the most trainees drop out. It is not uncommon for 75 per cent of the course to be gone by day eight. On some courses the drop-out rate is even higher.

During the second week, the soldiers are assessed on their individual navigational skills and their ability to work independently – operating alone. With no one to provide motivation, only the most highly disciplined and self-motivated soldiers are capable of passing this phase of the course.

There is also a roping component that is designed to test

those who suffer from a fear of heights. You don't need to enjoy yourself in order to move onto the final phase of the course, but you must complete all the activities to prove you are capable of operating outside of your comfort zone.

The last four or five days are the most exacting. Those who remain are divided into teams and sent from one gruelling activity to another. The men are subjected to enormous physical activity and at the same time are deprived of food and sleep. When soldiers are running on empty, who of them remains team-focused and who looks out just for themselves? Men who sneak into the bush to sleep, who volunteer themselves for the less arduous tasks or who fail to contribute to the team are soon identified as non-team-players and usually fail the course. The SAS requires high-performing personnel who can remain team-oriented regardless of what is going on around them.

It's impossible to determine how many soldiers will be left at the end. On some courses, up to 20 per cent of the applicants might complete the course, while on others there will be fewer than five per cent. I know of one course where just one officer and four soldiers remained. On average, only five per cent of soldiers who apply and 10 per cent of soldiers who attend the course make it into the SAS.

The directing staff (DS) who assess the trainees are predominantly senior SAS soldiers who hold the rank of sergeant or above. The DS carry notebooks and continuously scribble down whatever they observe, whether it's positive or negative. At the end of each day the DS get together and discuss the performance of the trainees.

The trainees are assessed on their physical fitness and

endurance, integrity, self-discipline, motivation, ability to work with others, acceptance of responsibility, leadership potential, stress management and work ethic. All comments by the DS are recorded in a trainee's personal file.

At the end of the course, the DS will meet and discuss the attributes of each trainee. The documentary evidence that was collected throughout the course will be closely scrutinised and a decision will be made about whether a trainee shows potential – that is, whether they are suitable for further training and assessment. It's not uncommon for the DS to disagree about soldiers' potential; when this occurs, it's the senior instructor (SI) who makes the final decision.

≡

Rog and I headed to Amberley Airfield on 21 March 1995. It was a sultry, cloudy afternoon. The following morning, with no expectations and oversized lunch boxes, we boarded a C130 transport aircraft. First stop Sydney, second stop Melbourne, third stop Adelaide, fourth stop RAAF Base Pearce, Western Australia.

Even the C130 was foreign to me – I had never flown in one before. At RAAF Base Rich-mond, in Sydney, dozens of soldiers from the 3rd and 5/7 Battalions boarded the aircraft. There were a few tense faces, but as a group they appeared far more relaxed than I

Packed and ready for
SAS selection.

felt. These guys were all regular soldiers. I looked them up and down, searching for strengths and any obvious signs of weakness. I wondered who would be there at the end. How fit were these guys? How many years had they been in the army?

Rog and I were both 21 years old. Most of these men appeared to be several years our senior. I noticed that there were officers, corporals, lance corporals and privates in the group – in fact, there were more soldiers with rank than without.

I remember three soldiers in particular from that flight. One had an adolescent face. He appeared to be only 18 or 19, was of slender build and probably weighed no more than 70 kilograms. I was surprised when I found out Craig was 21. He was there at the end.

Another guy, Mick, had dark skin and looked exceptionally fit. He had strong, large-veined arms and a thick neck. He wore dark sunglasses and had a peculiar grin. He too was there at the end.

I also noticed an olive-skinned man who seemed about 25 years of age. He looked fit and wiry. Brian was a full corporal and would go on to pass the course too.

I had to force myself to eat during the flight. I tried to sleep, both by dropping my head onto my knees and by pushing it back against the netting, but I couldn't. My body was anticipating something violent when the plane finally touched down. Sleep was never going to happen.

We landed at RAAF Base Pearce some 13 hours after departing Amberley. It was early in the evening and the sun was still up. I wondered what we'd be asked to do first. My imagination and pulse were running wild. Trying to second-guess what was coming created additional angst. I knew if I was to be there at the end I would have to settle down and back myself. There would probably be confusion and mayhem, perhaps a lot of yelling, but I decided I would react to whatever instructions were thrown my way and to nothing else. I wasn't going to be crippled by the nervous energy that had silenced the plane.

The rear ramp was lowered and hot air rushed into the aircraft. I felt nervous but in control. I saw a couple of SAS soldiers dressed in military fatigues standing on the tarmac behind the aircraft, their eyes focused on the C130. I knew they were SAS soldiers because they wore the trademark sandy beret. I had never seen an SAS soldier in the flesh before.

A confident man with a deep voice walked onto the aircraft. He was around six feet tall, of medium build and aged in his forties. Although I have a clear image of this man in my mind, including his expressionless face and confronting stare, I can't recall the precise words he spoke.

I'm very much a visual person. I'm often able to recall detailed information, mainly numbers and images, from my past. It's not always a good thing – my mind is cluttered with lots of useless information. Abstract things seem to be etched most deeply, such as the names of three Russian gymnasts from the 1988 Seoul Olympics – Dmitry Bilozerchev, Valeri Liukin and Vladimir Artemov. I saw their names on the bottom of the television screen in white bold writing, thought they were a little weird and have never forgotten them. Although this level of recall has been a useful skill, there are also ghastly images rolling around in my head that remain too clear. I wish this wasn't the case but I'm resigned to the fact that these memories will never fade, not even a little.

Upon exiting the aircraft at RAAF Base Pearce, we retrieved our equipment, were marched off the runway to a sparsely vegetated area and told to line up. We were facing the setting sun. As we stood at ease – our feet shoulder-width apart and our hands crossed behind our backs – the wing sergeant major (WSM) introduced himself and mentioned the names and positions of a couple of other people. We were told to remember these names.

He then had a question for us: 'Can anybody tell me the role of the SAS?'

There was no way I was going to open my mouth. But there were a number of soldiers who were keen to be recognised.

'Reconnaissance,' said one man.

'Yes, strategic reconnaissance. What else?' said the WSM.

'Counter-terrorism,' said another.

'What else?'

'Gather intelligence.'

And then came an answer that took us all by surprise.

'Kill people.'

'What was that?' said the WSM.

'Kill people,' said the man, even louder than before.

Even if someone truly believed such a thing, who in their right mind would say something so ridiculous? I thought to myself.

The WSM didn't miss a beat. 'Kill people, you think? Well, the last person I killed was someone who tried out for selection and didn't drink enough water.'

The WSM called out our names, and in groups of 12 we were ordered to grab our kits and jump on the trucks.

Once we were in, the rear canopy was tied down, leaving us sweating in the dark. The drivers drove fast, revving their vehicles hard. I looked at the other shadowy figures seated around me. Some heads were down, others flicked nervously to and fro, but no one said a word.

The truck stopped, the rear canopy was unlaced and we were told to get out. I saw a dozen soldiers swimming in a murky 25-metre pool, and dozens more lined up, waiting for their turn. We were told to remove our boots and everything from our pockets. My right ankle was heavily strapped with my foot locked at right-angles to my lower leg. I had wrongly presumed we would be doing a hell-march when we arrived in WA. I removed the strapping tape, revealing a tender, swollen joint.

We were required to swim 300 metres while dressed in military fatigues. The first 100 metres had to be freestyle, and after that any stroke was permissible. I recognised a regular army corporal from another Enoggera-based infantry battalion. He had a powerful build, was aged in his late twenties, and was the first in his squad to complete the swim.

This guy and I had crossed paths at least half a dozen times while training in Brisbane. On two occasions, while we were both weighed down with heavy packs, we walked past each other from opposite directions. It's obvious when someone is training for selection. I said: 'Good morning, Corporal,' but received no reply. I described the man to my platoon sergeant and he immediately knew who I was enquiring about.

'That's Jay,' he said. 'He's a real tough bastard, a jet' – army slang for a high-performing soldier. 'He'll piss it in.'

The next time I saw Jay he was shuffling down the mountain while I was stomping up. When we were no more than a metre apart, I looked him in the eye and said, 'G'day, Corporal.'

This time he sneered and shook his head, as if disgusted that a soldier with less than 12 months' experience in the army had the gall to attempt selection, or even to speak to him. *Arrogant prick*, I thought. I have never rated people who look down on others. It doesn't matter what you own, how many degrees you have, where you live, what you do for a job or what position you hold − if you're a wanker, your cock is all you've got, and all you're ever going to be.

Jay stood at the end of the pool, removed his shirt and waited for the second phase of the test: a 25-metre swim underwater while wearing camouflage pants. Once again Jay was first, breaking the surface looking composed and confident. At least half the guys in his squad failed this test.

Then it was my turn. I was then a pretty average swimmer, capable of swimming a kilometre in approximately 19 or 20 minutes. Swimming freestyle while dressed in military fatigues is especially tough, as you cannot glide. I was no Grant Hackett but had no trouble completing the first swim. I exited the pool behind two others and waited for the remainder of our squad to finish. Our next test was the 25-metre underwater swim.

I was surprised by how many guys were failing this test. I dived into the water knowing that if I was to fail, they would be pulling me from the water unconscious. I would not break the surface before I touched the opposite wall, no matter how much it hurt. I'd drink the pool dry and crawl along the bottom if I had to. I was excited and swam quickly, burning up lots of oxygen. The cam pants were a hindrance, and so too was the filthy water, which made it impossible to gauge the end. More than half of our squad failed the test, possibly because their nervous energy robbed them of oxygen. I was pleased to have passed.

We changed into dry fatigues and once again boarded the trucks. The stuffy darkness was less intimidating than before. Forty-five minutes later we arrived at Bindoon training area. I had no idea where we were. We were placed in squads and introduced to our directing staff (DS). I was in Eight Squad. Our DS, a fair man who had no intention of being a prick just for the sake of it, told us to ensure we thoroughly cleaned our eating utensils after each meal.

'Most of you guys have worked hard to get here. Don't let yourselves down with poor hygiene. If you get sick, even for a day, then you won't be able to cope with what's expected. If I find food or filth on anyone's KFS' – he meant our knife, fork and spoon – 'then you'll owe me 50 push-ups. Got it?'

'Yes, sir,' we replied.

We then assembled in the mess tent and were addressed by the senior instructor (SI), a captain who was in charge of the course.

'Men, welcome to the 1/95 SASR selection course. You are all going to be challenged, so I would like to offer you some words of encouragement.'

I leaned forward, keen to embrace any advice on offer.

'But none comes to mind,' the SI said, turning his back and walking away.

Talk about an anticlimax. It was a remarkable comment that took me completely by surprise.

We were sent to bed at 2300 hours. Our accommodation comprised lines of hootchies – two ground sheets joined together, draped over a piece of rope and staked at the corners. We slept on stretcher beds. There were two men to a hootchie and 12 to 16 men in each squad.

At midnight we were woken for a fire drill. We were also informed that day one had just begun. Yesterday, which in reality was just a couple of minutes ago, was just an admin day.

On Thursday 23 March 1995, I scribbled in my diary: 'Worst night sleep ever.' Quite a surprising comment, considering I wasn't cold or in threat of losing my life. Fear of the unknown well surpasses reality. I checked my watch and it was 0400 hours. I decided to get up early and have a shave. *This could save me some time later*, I thought.

≡

When I reflect on other experiences I've had – especially midnight road moves I trialled in Anbar province, Iraq, when I was running the security component of a reconstruction project – I can see I learnt to deal with stressful situations quite differently.

After being heavily scrutinised by the suits in London about my decision to hit the roads at night without any night-fighting capability (weapon lasers and night-vision goggles), I knew I would come under fire from above if we were hit and lives or assets were lost. But I knew that the US marines with whom we were collocated were being mauled three times a day on the roads around Haditha

Dam. I was aware that command and control, as well as trying to vector in support assets, would be far more difficult during the hours of darkness, but in order to dodge the insurgent bombs, it was a risk I was willing to take.

Lying on a warm asphalt surface at Alasad Airbase while waiting for the most suitable departure time – 0100 hours – I had no trouble dropping off to sleep. Sure, I was anxious, but over the years I had learnt to control my thoughts in order to be able to sleep when required. I knew that the return trip to Jordan, taking 10 or 11 hours, would be mentally demanding, so a couple of hours sleep were vital if I was to remain focused. We never did get hit at night.

≡

At 0545, my clean-shaven face was tucked deep in my sleeping bag when a song from the movie *Pulp Fiction* – 'Stuck In the Middle With You' – screamed out of a large set of speakers that were positioned on the fringe of our hootchies. This incited mayhem; some guys ran off to the bathrooms to shave, others frantically threw on their military fatigues, others yelled questions – 'What's the dress? What do we wear?' – while a few men just stood up and waited.

The words 'PT kit . . . dress is PT kit' were passed down the lines. PT kit comprised joggers, black shorts and a white T-shirt with your surname written on the front and back. We were split into two groups and told that we would be doing a BFA – a basic fitness assessment. The BFA was the standard fitness test for the Australian military. Group one would complete the five-kilometre run (at own pace), while group two – my group – would perform a push-up/sit-up test.

For this test, each soldier was required to do 60 push-ups to a cadence – no more, no less. I felt pretty confident. I knew I was capable of pumping out double that number in a two-minute period if required. Up to a dozen soldiers were told to stop because of poor technique. During the sit-up test, the corporal physical training instructor (PTI) berated a man who struggled to do 20 sit-ups. The required standard was 100.

'Jellyneck, did you do any preparation at all for this course?'

'Yes, sir.'

'Bullshit! What are you doing here? You can't even do 20 sit-ups. Did you follow the three-month training program?'

'Umm, yes, sir. Parts of it.'

'Parts of it! If you didn't follow the program, and it is obvious you didn't, then you have no chance of passing this course. And you've probably taken the position of someone who really wanted to be here. Do you think you should continue?'

'Yes, sir.'

'If I were you I would seriously consider my volunteer status. You're a disgrace.'

The PTI was not an abusive man, just passionate. I would later get to know him very well. Kane (my training partner in the Regiment) and I had many hardcore training sessions with this guy. He was a freak with a ridiculous set of arms. And they weren't bloated, unpractical, body-builder arms that clag out after one set of chin-ups. These guns could pump out five sets of 20 as a warm-up. Weighing in at 90 kilograms, he was a tremendous athlete. A testament to this was his ability to win the first *Gladiator* television series. At work he ran a mean circuit, but our troop generally ran our own training.

After completing the sit-up test, we moved to the start line for the five-kilometre run. Guys from the first group had been streaming in for five minutes, then, to my surprise, Jay the corporal – the guy I'd seen in training – crossed the line in a time of over 22 minutes. Hunched over and sucking in the big ones, he no longer looked confident and composed. I'm not sure if his time was good enough to pass, but that was the last I saw of him. The next day, I noticed his bed space was empty. The jet, the tough bastard, the man who would piss it in, was out of there.

I completed the run in a time of 18 minutes and eight seconds. There were a few gazelles who kicked my arse, but I was content with my time.

After breakfast we were lined up in squads on a gravel parade ground. We were ordered to lay out our ground sheets and remove everything from our packs, webbing and echelon bags. We were also required to remove all our clothing except our underwear and hats. The air was hot and dry. I felt anxious; sweat trickled down my ribs and the soles of my feet stuck to my groundsheet. A member of the directing staff read out a list of items, one at a time, that we were instructed to hold in the air. Anyone who was missing an item had their name recorded for failing to assimilate simple instructions. They were punished later.

The DS then inspected our packs, webbing and the pockets of all our clothing to ensure we didn't have anything that wasn't on the list. If soldiers declared the items then there would be no problem. If guys were hiding things – such as food or specialist equipment – and it was found, then they would be removed from the course due to a lack of integrity. I had spent considerable time waterproofing all my equipment. The DS removed each item from its snap-lock bag with care and precision. They methodically inspected the seams of my clothing, looked for hidden compartments in my pack and thumbed their way over every inch of my belt. They displayed no emotion.

In the afternoon, two physical training instructors smashed us with a weights circuit. I enjoyed it – I was being paid to do what I loved: hard training. Our efforts were heavily scrutinised by up to 10 directing staff. We were expected to hold nothing back. For me, the most painful exercise was the tyre shoulder press. By the end of the session, most guys struggled to raise their hands above their heads, me included.

The following morning we were told to dress in military fatigues, grab our rifles and weigh our webbing – it had to weigh a minimum of eight kilograms. There was a lot of yelling and guys were running everywhere. In squads, we were marched down a track and informed that we were doing a webbing run test. The required dress was boots, cams, webbing and rifle. To pass the test, we had to complete the 3.2-kilometre course in less than 16 minutes. We were not permitted to wear a watch.

Whatever your fitness level, a webbing run is one of the

most painful and difficult physical tests in the military. The added weight sees your legs heavy with lactic acid after the first 200 metres, and your heart rate will soon be operating at its maximum beats per minute. Just like running up a steep sandhill, there is no cruise mode, even for guys who can complete the run in 12 or 13 minutes. It is a grind that burns your lungs, calves and thighs from start to finish. We weren't informed of our times, simply given a pass or fail. I finished sixth. The 20 soldiers who failed the run were given one more chance. Those who failed a second time were removed from the course.

This type of fitness – battle fitness – is critical for SAS soldiers. If SAS soldiers are in heavy contact against a numerically superior force, then they must be able to break contact while heavily laden with equipment. The stress upon their bodies – and minds – will be extreme. It's vastly different from throwing on a set of joggers and running fast. A strong will is required to embrace the pain and to continue pushing when your legs are begging to be able to walk. Those who choose to walk are those who fail.

I'd pushed hard on the run so I struggled through breakfast. I was a bit nauseated and forcing the food down only exacerbated the feeling. We then completed a navigation exercise before lunch. In the heat of the afternoon, we boarded trucks and departed. I was certain we'd be doing the airfield run, a punishing session with a huge reputation. But this wasn't the case.

We assembled in a hangar and were briefed. 'Okay, men, yesterday you completed the BFA – the basic fitness assessment. There is nothing special about that – everyone in the military has to do it. You'll now complete the special-forces

BFA. I'm sure you'll find it a little more challenging.'

The first test was 60 push-ups. *Easy enough*, I thought. I was wrong. The cadence was agonisingly slow: just one push-up every four or five seconds. Guys who broke form were told to stand up. There were many. After 50 push-ups in three and a half minutes, my thighs began to spasm. This pissed me off. I made it to 60.

The second test was maximum chin-ups.

'When I say "adopt the position",' the PTI said, 'the front row of men will grab the bar − overgrasp or under-grasp − and hang at full extension. On the command "go" you will complete one set of maximum chin-ups. Are there any questions?'

Wisely, no one answered.

'Adopt the position.'

On this command, one man, whose thick arms were covered in tattoos, jumped on to the bar and began a frenzy of chin-ups. The directing staff repeatedly yelled at him to stop but he didn't seem to notice. He had completed 13 or 14 before he stopped. The others were made to hang at full extension while the eager man was counselled.

'You failed to assimilate simple instruction. None of those chin-ups will count.' This was followed by silence, then: 'Go!'

The man managed another 10. He was credited with six because of poor technique.

I was in the fifth line to begin and chose undergrasp. I completed 20 but was credited with just 16. I was not happy with this. After the course, I trained up and set myself a minimum standard of 25. A few years later, Kane,

Mick and I were invited for a session with the Regimental PTI. We managed 126 in five sets, with a five-minute break in between each set, but this was as good as it got. Clawing your way up the side of an oil rig in the middle of a Bass Strait winter can be dangerous. For an SAS diver, chin-ups are like insurance – you pay up front and collect during times of need.

The next challenge was 100 unsupported sit-ups, then we were taken outside and briefed on another test, a 2.6-kilometre run. We were wearing PT kit and carrying our rifles. We would only be informed whether we had passed or failed the run at the finish line. The course, a hot gravel track, ascended a series of ridges. I finished in the top eight with a time of nine minutes and 54 seconds. Three-quarters of the course failed to make the cut-off time of 10 minutes and 30 seconds. The heat was unbearable. I felt sick.

Surely that's it, I thought. But this was SAS selection, so of course there was more to come.

We were told to start running up the track to a parked truck. The first 20 guys were to jump in the back, and everyone else was to keep on running. We had no idea how far we'd be expected to run. I was the 23rd or 24th guy to the truck, and my heart rate was through the roof. I had missed the cut so I kept running. Those who made it to the truck were soon yelled at and told to get out and get going too.

We ascended false crest after false crest. I longed for the finish line. I tried to anticipate how far, realistically, we would be made to run. I was thinking 20 kilometres. There were a couple of drink stations but the white plastic cup of water at each one was barely enough to moisten my parched throat. I knew I was overheating, and my head began to ache.

The red, gravelly track continued on and up. My legs felt weary and my brain like a fried egg. We ran for 11 kilometres, all the way back to camp. When I arrived, guys were guzzling from 20-litre jerry cans. I had a turn but only managed two or three gulps before I thought I was going to vomit. My legs and hands were shaking; I was definitely suffering from heat exhaustion.

We showered and readied ourselves for dinner. There was no down time. Everything was rushed, every moment was hectic. At the completion of the third day we had lost almost half the course. At least 60 or 70 guys were gone. Some had suffered injuries and some were asked to leave, but most left because they'd had enough.

I couldn't eat that evening. I dry-retched after putting a single piece of chicken in my mouth. The lasagne fared no better. So I filled my stomach with fluid and hoped my headache would fade soon. I went to bed feeling like shit. But I had made it to the end of day three. *Just 17 or 18 days to go*, I thought.

Day four began with a 90-minute PT session. In groups of five we were given a large truck tyre to guide around the gravel tracks of Bindoon. Our team decided to have two guys pushing from behind, a guy to the left and right to steer, and one off to the side resting.

On a flat road it worked pretty well. Going uphill was hard work but the tyre was easy to control. Downhill was another story. Up to eight hands would be pressed down on the rubber as the tyre gained momentum, in a feeble attempt to slow it down. Most guys lost a fair portion of skin off their palms. Rogue tyres sometimes broke free, only slowing down when they collected the group in front.

There was no shortage of prying eyes watching our every move. The DS constantly pulled notebooks out of their trouser pockets and scribbled away. I tried to take no notice. I placed my efforts and attention solely on the task we were completing. *If I do this right*, I thought, *everything else should take care of itself*. Trying to second-guess what someone thinks of your efforts is a waste of energy. And the thought of kissing someone's arse, especially in the SAS, never entered my mind.

=

In the Regiment I socialised with guys I liked, regardless of their rank or position. Trooper, corporal, sergeant, warrant officer or 'Rupert' (an officer) – what did it matter?

I remember chatting to Todd (a good mate) and Buzz (our team commander) at a function at the Gratwick Club – the SAS watering hole at Campbell Barracks. A drunken sergeant approached us and said: 'When you guys are finished kissing your team commander's arse, I'd like to have a chat to him.'

His comment incensed me, almost to the point where I thought about landing one on the prick's chin. Todd was an angry bastard at the best of times, and I could see he was thinking something similar. We'd only been in the troop for 12 months, but as far as we were concerned, we were free to talk to whomever we liked. Buzz was a sergeant, but so what? He was also a mate.

Buzz saw our faces change. As a good leader does, he took care of it. 'Hey, these boys are fucking solid and I'm chatting to them. The Gratto's their pub, not ours.'

Thankfully, there wasn't much of that sort of attitude in the Regiment. The only pecking order that most guys cared about was performance.

Am I anti-authoritarian? I don't think so. I just don't believe that rank or social standing gives you the right to speak down to others. Condescending language is the language of the inept – bigoted souls with something to prove.

≡

The guys of Eight Squad were team players. From the outset we all had a strong sense of camaraderie. Many squads had already folded because of withdrawals, resulting in the merging of two or more groups. Our squad, with only a couple of withdrawals, remained intact.

After breakfast on day four we were driven to Julimar. The trucks stopped and let us off, we threw on our packs and webbing, then the trucks drove on again. It was hot and the sun was burning into the shoulders of our camouflaged shirts.

'Follow me,' ordered the SI, taking off down the track.

The pace was hectic. After 15 minutes the lead group of a dozen soldiers was told to stop and join the back of the line. Twice I worked my way to the front, only to be sent to the back. I then decided to stay in the middle. The pace remained fast, and some soldiers struggled to keep up.

After 45 minutes I removed a water bottle from my webbing to take a drink, but my ankle rolled on the side of a large tree root. I had not re-strapped it after the pool swim, which was a decision I would come to rue.

Fuck, I thought. The pain was pretty intense. Someone helped me to my feet and I kept walking. For five minutes I felt nauseated and my ankle throbbed, lacking stability.

Ten minutes later I rolled it again. *That's that*, I thought. *Only made it to bloody day four.* I tried to stand up but my ankle couldn't bear my weight.

My DS — a fair man — approached me and asked what had happened. He could see the distress on my face. 'Look, mate,' he said. 'I reckon those trucks are only a couple of hundred metres up the road. Reckon you can make it?'

'Yes, sir,' I replied as I got to my feet.

Then the WSM arrived, and he was not so positive. 'Would you like to remove yourself from the course, trainee?'

'No, sir.'

'Then why were you sitting down?'

'I rolled my ankle, sir.'

He didn't believe me. 'I think you should re-evaluate your volunteer status.'

'No, sir, I will never remove myself from the course. I damaged my ankle prior to selection and got rid of my crutches three days before the course.' I had no reason to lie. All he had to do was check my medical documents.

The WSM called a medic over.

'He's done a decent job on this,' the medic said. 'It's already bruised.'

'If you strap it it'll be okay,' I said.

'Your ankle's gonna swell — strapping tape might inhibit your circulation,' said the medic.

'His ankle's already swollen. Strap it up and see how it goes,' said the WSM.

The medic used the best part of an entire roll to secure my ankle. It was now impossible for it to roll. I rejoined my squad, which was just a couple of hundred metres up the track.

That afternoon we were sent in pairs on a navigational exercise. My partner was a signaller named Cassidy, an intelligent and genuine guy. I was disappointed that he wasn't there at the end of the course. We returned to our squad base location, as ordered, after last light.

'How's your ankle?' enquired my DS.

'No problem,' I said.

'Of course there's no problem, but how is it?'

'Fine, sir.'

'Look after it tomorrow. That goes for all of you,' he added to the group. 'Air out your feet. You all know you've got your 20-clicker —' our 20-kilometre pack march — 'coming up. If you don't make the cut-off time then you've got Buckley's of passing the retest. You've really only got one shot.'

Our DS had a different approach from the others. He was keen to offer encouragement if he thought you deserved it. That evening our squad members got to know each other a little better. Our DS kept the conversation going with a few questions, but he left most of the talking to the guys.

The next morning, with a second list of checkpoints to navigate to, Cassidy and I headed off. We pushed hard through the morning, which meant we could take a bit of time in the middle of the day to dry out our sleeping equipment. Throughout the afternoon we managed our speed to ensure we reached the rendezvous on time. We had made it to the end of day five.

Although we'd been told that day one of the course only began the day after we arrived, it was really a ploy to unsettle us. After the long flight, the angst of expectation, the swim test and then being woken up at midnight after barely an hour's sleep, the guys were feeling shattered. To then be told that day one had only just began was like sprinting over the finish line of a marathon and then being told you still had two kilometres to go. But the SAS wants men who aren't discouraged by extended finish lines.

As you near the end of a deployment, most soldiers are excited to get home and see their families. At first you might be told: 'The deployment will be six months, and then you'll all be home for Christmas.' But with two weeks to go, things change. Instead of hiding next to the chimney to scare Santa on Christmas Eve, you are hanging out in Afghanistan or Iraq because your deployment has been extended by three months.

Colleen abseiling.

You then have a choice: you can be a sook, or you can put it behind you and crack on with business. In my experience, SAS (and army) wives are some of the toughest women around. My wife had more than a decade of extended finish lines. Sure, she was often disap-pointed, but not once did she give me any grief about it. If something is out of your control, then worrying about it is pointless.

≡

Day six, Monday 27 March 1995, was a big day. We were woken earlier than normal. The usual nervous mayhem of not knowing what's going on buzzed through our hootchies like a swarm of bees on adrenaline.

'Dress is cams, webbing and packs,' someone yelled. 'Weigh your packs – we're doing the 20-clicker.'

I ran to the scales to weigh my gear. We were told that our packs must weigh a minimum of 20 kilograms and our webbing at least eight kilograms. But we weren't permitted to remove weight if we were over. My pack and webbing weighed 26.5 kilograms and 9.5 kilograms. With my rifle, I'd be running with 40 kilos.

We marched to the start line and assembled in squads, which were dispatched at 60-second intervals. One by one the groups departed. Some men walked, some ran, most shuffled. Eight Squad would be the second-last to leave, seven minutes behind the first group. The seven minutes would be deducted from our times at the end.

I had no intention of doing this test again. A couple of guys in our squad had talked about doing it together. *No way*, I thought. This was an individual test. With the exception of any hills and drinks breaks, my plan was to shuffle the entire way.

Finally, it was our turn to leave. My heart was already beating hard when we lined up. We were told to go, and go

I did. I was determined to pass this test the first time. For the first couple of minutes my legs felt heavy, but I soon settled into a rhythm. I was the first from Eight Squad to reach the trailing members of Seven Squad.

'Hey, take it easy, mate – you'll burn out,' someone yelled.

I felt pretty good so didn't take any notice. I ran for 20 minutes, before slowing down to take a few sips of water. Trying to hold your breath and drink when your body is craving oxygen is always a struggle. I occasionally got it wrong, coughing and spluttering as water was sucked into my lungs. I continued running before I put my water bottle away.

After an hour I had passed at least half the starters. I knew Rog was in Two Squad and I was looking forward to saying g'day. Fifteen minutes later I recognised his stocky frame shuffling along the track some 200 metres down the hill. I increased my efforts, running almost as fast as I could, and pulled alongside him. He wasn't wearing a hat, and streams of sweat ran down his face and neck.

'Hey, mate, I've been trying to catch you for the last 75 minutes,' I said. 'How're you feeling?'

'Yeah, okay. What about you?' he said.

'Same. Feet are burning, though.'

'Tell me about it.'

'I'm gonna get going,' I said. 'Smash it, mate!'

'Grab me a beer when you get there,' said Rog with a smile on his face.

I picked up the pace and didn't stop running until I came to a steeper section of track. Halfway up, two guys shuffled past me. *What the fuck?* I thought I was going hard.

Except for the SI, who wasn't carrying a pack, these were the only guys to pass me. I must admit, it did piss me off.

I saw several DS at a drinks station halfway up the hill to my front. There was also a man with a video camera. I filled up my water bottles and followed the track to the right. I knew there were at least four guys in front of me.

The track wound its way up the mountain. I stopped shuffling and walked fast. The sound of approaching footsteps behind me took me by surprise. *I don't believe it – not someone else overtaking me*, I thought. I glanced over my shoulder and started running when I saw it was the SI.

'Are you coming first, trainee Fennell?'

He knows my name – surely that can't be good. So much for being the grey man. 'No, sir. I'm the first member of Eight Squad, but I know of at least four others in front.'

'Why do you want to be an SAS soldier?'

'I love soldiering and I want to take it to the highest level, sir.'

'What will you do if you don't pass the course?'

'I'm not considering that option, sir.'

'That's a bold statement.'

'No, sir. If I fail the course then I will be discharged from full-time service.'

'Why's that?'

I then explained the ready reserve.

'Well, don't worry about that. The regular army can keep the fodder. We're after thinking soldiers,' he said, smiling.

The SI didn't say a lot, but his body language and comments appeared positive. I reached the top of the hill. 'Excuse me, sir,' I said, 'I'm going to double-time.'

'Don't let me hold you back,' he said.

I started running. Twenty metres later the SI ran past me and soon disappeared. *Bastard*, I thought. My feet felt like they were on fire. I kept on running.

I looked at my watch and thought that the end would have to be close. I reached another water station and, this time, the DS recorded my name. *This was strange*, I thought.

A kilometre later, a DS approached me and asked, 'Trainee, how far do you think you have to go?'

'I'm not sure – it could be another five kilometres,' I said.

'Five kilometres?' he said, surprised. 'How's your time and space?'

'I believe the last water station was approximately 20 kilometres, sir. By my estimates, I should have already finished.'

The DS smiled and nodded his head. 'Fair enough.'

Around the corner was the finish line, and I was eighth to cross. We had to provide our trainee and squad numbers.

'Trainee 67, Eight Squad,' I said.

The sergeant PTI, a short, balding man with an athletic build and dark hairy legs, looked up from his time sheet and said, 'Eight Squad? Well done. That's an excellent time. Go and dump your pack over there and get yourself a drink.'

I removed my boots and socks to inspect my feet. Apart from a large blood blister underneath my right big toe, my feet were fine. My ankle, still heavily strapped, felt like it was being strangled. I made a slight cut in the strapping, which did relieve the pressure.

A medic came to inspect my feet. 'I can drain that blood blister for you and pump it full of antiseptic to help dry it out, if you like?'

'Yes please,' I said.

He drained the blister, filled a five-millilitre syringe with a yellowish fluid and smiled. 'I forgot to tell you – this shit really stings.'

I did my best to show no emotion, but my big toe was totally freaking out. My diary entry that night said it all: 'Ouch, ouch, ouch, instant fucking burn.'

I threw on a fresh set of socks, stretched my legs and tried to eat a cold bacon and egg sandwich. I was stoked to have passed the test.

That afternoon, we were tested on our basic signalling, medical and weapon skills. Test one: set up an ANPR 77 radio and use correct ratel (radio telecommunications) procedures. Test two: treat an array of medical conditions, from heat illness and leg fractures to snake bites. Test three: basic weapon handling.

Three hours later, the corporal PTI with the massive guns smashed the hell out of us with metal pipes. He didn't bash us with them – it was a weights session – but I probably would have preferred it to the 90-minute flogging our shoulders and arms received.

At midnight we received a lesson on Morse code. *Alpha – dit-dah; Bravo – dah-dit-dit-dit; Charlie – dah-dit-dah-dit . . .*

≡

I woke early the next morning. My first thought was: *Made it to day seven.* It was now Tuesday 28 March. My legs, hips, lower back and shoulders were as stiff as they'd ever been. I no longer tried to anticipate how many days there were to go. Thinking too far ahead was dangerous. When things became more challenging, I even broke my day up into two-hourly blocks. *Made it to 1000 hours; midday; 1400 hours . . .*

The day began with another physical test – a 15-kilometre hell run. Once again, our dress was cams, webbing (eight kilograms), boots and rifle. It was less than 24 hours since we'd completed the 20-kilometre pack run, and most guys were heavily fatigued.

After two kilometres my legs loosened up and I maintained a steady cadence. At approximately 10 kilometres, while running up a sharp gradient, I noticed a sniper from the 3rd Battalion ahead. Battalion snipers are some of the most highly respected soldiers. I increased my pace and caught him up. We were at a similar physical standard; we'd consistently finished near each other on the previous physical tests.

'Hey, mate, how're your legs?' he asked.

'Pretty fatigued,' I replied.

'Let's smash it to the top of this hill,' he said.

'Yeah, let's do it.'

Halfway up, he said: 'Keep going, mate; I'm gonna walk for a bit.'

I felt okay so I continued on. I finished in fourth place in a time of 97 minutes and six seconds. My legs were shattered. We'd been allowed 100 minutes to complete the run, and more than half the course had failed.

As soon as I had finished, I felt my legs begin to tighten. I pulled out a water bottle, took small sips and stretched. I saw Rog come in. His legs were also starting to cramp, so we helped each other stretch, offering words of encouragement. I stood up, spun around and noticed the SI standing directly behind me. Wearing a dark set of sunglasses and a blank face, he'd been listening to our conversation. It was slightly unnerving – this time he gave away nothing.

We were then ordered to line up and were told we would be running the 15 kilometres back to Bindoon training camp. *Holy shit*, I thought. My legs were hammered.

A couple of guys remained seated. They'd had enough and voluntarily removed themselves from the course. The rest of us began the march. Five hundred metres down the road there were several trucks. We were told to get on and were driven back to camp.

≡

The first week of the course was designed to wear us down, to remove our protective shells and expose the quality of the flesh beneath, to weed out the majority of those who were unsuitable. After just those seven days, there were 80 or 90 empty stretchers at base camp. Seeing this enhanced my self-belief. The intense physical testing ensures that applicants are at the minimum physical standard required, but it also deliberately wears them out, so that their performance in the more challenging phases of the course will reveal their true persona – what lies beneath the surface.

After breakfast, it was time for more mind games. The SI assembled the course and told everyone that he had lost his compass and that we had to help him find it. We were also told to bring our packs and webbing. The SI's pack did not cut into his shoulders the same way that ours did. Nor was he hunched over, which suggested to me that his pack was filled with perhaps just a bulky sleeping bag and a pillow. Holding a map upside down, he began walking down the road. He was a tall man with long legs – this guy could stomp hard.

The pace was frantic, and within 20 minutes soldiers were strung out over hundreds of metres. The SI told our lead group of eight or nine soldiers to keep going, and to stop in the shade some 200 metres up the track. For the first time on the course, he also offered some words of encouragement. 'Well done, men. I'll be back in a few minutes.'

As soon as the SI left us, one soldier – a guy who was struggling to keep pace – vented: 'Fucking slow it down, guys . . .' His whining antics continued all the way to the shade.

The SI returned a few minutes later and it was on again. I was up the front and on his left side. I struggled to match his stride and so had to continuously break into a shuffle to keep pace. It was a hot day and the dry air stripped our mouths and throats of moisture. Fifteen minutes later the SI once again stopped our lead group. To say I was relieved was an understatement.

He stormed off and when he came back, his voice was terse. 'As you can see,' he said, 'I have split the course into three groups: those who are serious, those who are undecided, and those who are wasting our time. Group one, you will march with me. We've cut away the crap, now keep up.'

Never have I tried to walk so fast. We had been marching for about six kilometres when the SI glanced at the guys to his left and right and arrogantly increased the pace. This continued for another two kilometres.

I was locked in a mental battle with the SI, although he didn't know it. *I bet you've got a pillow in your pack, you fucker. I'd like to see how you'd go with a bit of weight in there.* I was determined to break him, just once, but that was never going to happen. Whenever I angled in front a little he stepped it out. *Bastard!*

I then began to fight my own mind. One part of me was pissed off that I'd gone to the front, because now the SI would notice if I fell back. But each time I thought about dropping back, my pride gave me a kick up the arse. Physically, however, I was on the limit. I knew I could only continue that pace for another minute or two.

Fortunately, the SI slowed down. 'Well done, men. Have a seat in the shade.'

Upon reflection, it was probably silly to flog myself like that. There were still two weeks to go. But thoughts of self-preservation never entered my mind. In hindsight, I've often wondered whether I should have approached that first week differently – whether I ought to have saved myself a little. But my answer remains an emphatic no. I was determined to give an honest account of myself.

I was naive for thinking that, just because the SI had said 'well done', the march was over. A tough-looking man, an SAS sergeant with a solid build and gruff voice, told our group to line up on the track. 'Can you guys run?' he asked.

So the nightmare continued. *A damn tag team*, I thought. The sergeant left the track, so we fell into single file behind him and ran through the bush. I was second or third in line. I was initially apprehensive that I would roll my ankle, but as my thighs became charged with lactic acid, my worries disappeared as quickly as the fluid from my body. It was stifling, and the speed ridiculous. Once again, my legs screamed at my mind to slow down. My mind's reply: *Suck it up, you freaking pussies*.

We ran for 800 metres. The sergeant was also surprisingly positive. 'Well done,' he said. 'Drop your packs and take a seat. The trucks will be here soon.'

My legs were dead. With shaking hands, I removed a bottle from my webbing, unscrewed the cap and sucked it dry. My hands soon settled down. *What's next?*

4

WEEK TWO: OPERATING ALONE

A t midday on day seven we began a solo 36-hour navigational exercise. On the way to my fifth check-point, after about six hours of hard going, I was soaked in perspiration and was walking like my testicles were the size of soccer balls. I dropped my trousers and saw that my groin and inner thighs were weeping, chafed raw. We weren't permitted to wear bike pants or skins underneath our fatigues, as all applicants had to be assessed under identical conditions.

I didn't have time to stop so, without taking off my pack and webbing, I pulled a clasp knife out of my pocket and sliced my soggy underwear down the sides. Watery blood trickled down my inner thighs. 'Man, you'd never get sex looking like that,' I said aloud. I threw my under-wear into a magazine pouch, pulled up my pants, fastened my belt and kept walking. That night I smothered my groin in army foot powder. It did relieve the stinging sensation.

The following morning I dug a hole, buried my under-wear and continued on. In the early hours of the afternoon

I reached the final rendezvous, my ninth checkpoint. There were eight or nine guys who arrived before me. The first couple were experienced soldiers, members of the 1st Battalion.

A couple of hours later the WSM briefed the remaining course applicants. 'We're sending you all out again because you failed to complete enough checkpoints by night. You'll all be given the grid coordinates at your drop-off locations.'

In groups of up to a dozen soldiers, we were squashed into the back of a 'sixby' – a six-wheel Land Rover – and driven to our individual start locations. Each time the vehicle stopped, a soldier was told to get off and given an eight-figure grid reference. My trainee number was the third to be called out.

The man responsible for providing the grid coordinates was my original DS. 'Prepare to copy your grid.'

I grabbed a notebook out of my pocket and told him I was ready. He then read out the coordinates.

'What's your bearing?'

I told him.

He nodded his head. 'Good. Look, mate, you're doing really well. Keep it up.'

I calculated that I would be traversing some thick and undulating terrain, and that the distance to my first checkpoint was 5.3 kilometres. Navigation by night or by day uses exactly the same principles, but it's easy to wander off your bearing during the transition from light to dark. The tree you line up in your compass can quickly disappear in the shadows.

After 45 minutes I had travelled 2.8 kilometres. I sat down, had something to eat and – following the advice I had received – waited for darkness to devour the landscape. Twenty minutes later I resumed my final 2.5 kilometres. I hit the ground several times, tripping over logs and rocks; once I slid down a gully. I had a small torch on a lanyard around my neck, but it stopped working after the gully incident so I used the light on my watch to illuminate my map and pace counter. My destination was a creek junction. According to my map, the vegetation was going to be dense. It was.

With 50 metres to go, I peered deep into the darkness, searching for a glow stick or any sign of light. I knew one of the DS would be at the checkpoint. I saw nothing – just shadows with contrasting degrees of blackness. Eighty metres later I had still not found my checkpoint. The ground rose sharply to my right, so after consulting my map I turned left and pushed deeper towards the creek. *It's gotta be close*, I thought. *Trust your compass and paces.*

I lost my balance and fell again. As I got to my knees, I noticed a flicker of light. But when I stood up it was gone. I leant forward and there it was – a faint glow further up the creek. As I closed in, the glow became brighter – it was a checkpoint.

When I got there I half-expected to be told I was at the wrong one. I was given another eight-figure grid reference, before being told to move 100 metres into the bush and lie up for the night. I was permitted to leave at first light.

The following morning I headed off for my eleventh and final checkpoint. When I reached the target – the junction of two tracks – I called in my coordinates and was informed to wait in place. A vehicle would be dispatched to pick me up.

Over the radio I heard that half a dozen trainees had become 'geographically embarrassed' – a fancy term for being lost. One was told to move in a northerly direction until he reached the main road. During the night, this guy had lost his map. He was a Battalion sniper; he completed the course but was not accepted.

While waiting for the truck to arrive, I checked my notebook and calculated how far I had travelled during the two navigational exercises. The total was 43 kilometres.

≡

Later that afternoon – day nine – we had our last 90-minute session with the PTIs. It was one to remember. We were divided into teams and given another truck tyre to push around. *Great*, I thought. *More skin shredded from my palms. Oh well, I don't have the energy to masturbate, so what does it matter?*

The second phase of the session comprised a circuit of chin-ups, push-ups and sit-ups. The finale was 10 minutes of gruelling abdominals. We pushed through the burn, hit that numb feeling and kept on going. Then the muscles ceased contracting. When this happened, we were ordered to rest with another set of chin-ups.

Friday 31 March was a roping day and, according to my diary, was a 'great day'. After the previous nine days, our bodies welcomed the lower intensity. But for some soldiers, climbing a 10-storey tower and completing a 60-metre traverse – sliding along a rope suspended between two towers – was utter anguish. If this freaked them out, then I'm sure the next exercises – a forward rappel, then a 10-storey building climb and emergency stop – were enough to push them over the edge.

You don't have to be a base-jumping adrenaline addict to be an SAS soldier. But you must be able to overcome your fears in order to get the job done. The applicants who didn't complete these activities were removed from the course.

That evening, the 50 of us who remained were jammed into the back of a couple of seven-tonne trucks and driven to Lancelin, a coastal military training area 127 kilometres north of Perth.

≡

Besides being a team player, SAS soldiers are selected on their ability to work independently – to operate alone. Accordingly, the next phase of the course was a four-day individual navigation exercise. Each soldier was required to complete as many checkpoints and travel as many kilometres as he could.

We weren't told when the activity would finish or how many kilometres we were expected to cover – it was a test of personal discipline and self-belief. How hard will guys push themselves when there is no one around to make them? We were given guidelines, one of which was that there was to be no walking on tracks. If a soldier was caught moving along a track, he'd immediately be removed from the course for a lack of moral integrity. The WSM was so clear about this that I was almost too shit-scared even to cross over a track, let alone parallel one.

In one sense, I was relieved to have made it this far and looked forward to spending four days alone. I planned to rest for 10 minutes each hour and break for 30 minutes during the hottest part of the day. I would walk until it got dark and then push on for another 30 to 45 minutes. How hard I pushed was up to me – I was responsible for shaping my own destiny.

It was a bit like rocking up to your office job and finding a note on your desk informing you that everyone else – including your boss – has been granted leave for the immediate future. You, however, are to begin working your way through 20 large boxes of paperwork, each box the equivalent of a week's normal work. You're not permitted to go home and you should sleep on the floor. It's summer, the air-conditioning has been turned off and your office is infested with thousands of flies. There's enough food to last you five days – nothing too exciting, of course. You'll be hungry, but you won't die from a lack of sustenance. When you choose to eat and sleep is up to you. And finally, there are to be no Google searches, no email and no phone calls – just you, your 20 boxes of paperwork and a few thousands flies. Oh, and there are a couple of snakes somewhere in the office – but don't be concerned. Although dugites are poisonous, they're not aggressive and should keep to themselves.

After four days alone, with no end in sight, how hard would you continue to push? On the SAS selection course, three boxes of paperwork would be deemed a solid effort, two and a half a fair effort, two boxes adequate and one box – the equivalent to a week's work in four days – a fail. Pack your bags, you're going back to the Battalion.

For safety, each man carried a radio and was required to send a daily message to confirm his location. Apart from the DS at the checkpoints, we were alone. In four days I saw only one other trainee; he was traversing a ridge over a kilometre away.

My first leg was 10.8 kilometres. When I was about halfway there, I stumbled into a small clearing and found two large green garbage bins. I lifted one of the lids and found it was brimming with marijuana. I called it in.

'Say again, trainee 67?'

'This is trainee 67. I have just found two bins filled with marijuana at grid reference –'

'Wait, wait out,' was the reply.

I then heard an older voice, a voice with greater authority. I confirmed my previous message and was ordered to remain where I was; they would send a vehicle to collect it. Ninety minutes later a six-wheel long-range patrol vehicle came into view. I showed them the pot, they put it in their vehicle and I continued on. I lost an hour and a half; it would probably have been quicker to sit down and smoke the lot.

On the way to checkpoint two, 16.8 kilometres away, I miscalculated how much water I would need to carry. Essentially, I was being a little softcock and tried to carry eight litres, rather than the 10 I should have. I then lost two litres when one of my bladders burst. As a consequence, I spent a very thirsty couple of hours crossing the sand dunes. The heat was extreme. While walking across the dunes, I thought: *If I screw up my navigation and can't locate the checkpoint, I could be in a bit of trouble here.* I was dizzy but still coherent. My tongue felt swollen, and the rear of my throat was as dry as the sand beneath my boots. I would never make this mistake again.

I've seen senior soldiers in the Regiment do this while

deployed on operations. When men are carrying up to 65 kilograms, the thought of leaving a water bottle or two empty can be tempting. Once it affected the operational security of our patrol. Anyone who has experienced extreme thirst – that painful sensation that dominates your every thought and makes you scared because you realise your body is starting to shut down – is reluctant to ever go there again. Fortunately, I had learnt my lesson early. The first thing I did when I reached the checkpoint was fill up my water bottles – all of them, all eight litres.

Negotiating the prickly saltbush and dealing with the flies tested my mental toughness. I wrote the following in my diary:

> *Had at least 200 flies on pack, body and face. Sun was intense; sweating, flies were attracted to fluid: nose, lips, corners of eyes and bleeding hands – disgusting bastards were relentless in their quest to feed. I reached the green terrain* [most extreme vegetation] *and movement was once again slow. Backs of hands were bleeding, shins and thighs red-raw from tearing through saltbush. Nearly went mental from flies. Wanted to scream but instead decided to sit down and kill flies for 20 minutes. Kept going, pushing through saltbush was extremely painful. Mental state severely tested.*

≡

If there was one guy who was jetting our course, from what I observed and heard from others, it was a particular soldier from the 1st Battalion. He was aged in his late twenties and had blitzed the previous navigational exercises.

My good mate Evo later told me that while he was having a break on our first nav exercise, he saw the guy charging through the bush.

'It was almost intimidating,' Evo told me. 'This guy was a machine. When I saw how hard he was going, I realised I had better lift my game so I packed up my things and got going. Seeing him motivated me to go harder.'

This guy's peers spoke of him as though he were a legend; he probably already was in the Battalion, where he'd been deployed to Somalia. He seemed like a good bloke – intelligent, personable and tough.

On our second day alone in the bush in Lancelin, I stopped to have something to eat and checked my radio to hear what was going on. I heard a deep, familiar voice – it belonged to the jet from the 1st Battalion. He was asking to be removed from the course. I couldn't believe it and turned up the volume.

Unlike others who had withdrawn, this man was asked numerous times whether he had thought about his decision. He was also asked if he was aware of the consequences, to which he replied: 'Yes, sir.'

Generally, anyone who requests to be removed from the course is never permitted to try again. In saying this, however, I'm aware of a couple of exceptions. If a soldier is relatively young then he might be given a second chance due to his lack of maturity or mental toughness. At 20, one is definitely not a boy, but might still be a little underdone in regards to being a bona fide man. Everyone is different and, depending on what they've experienced in life, some young men are mature beyond their years.

In Western society, life today is a little easier compared

to what previous generations lived through. My great-grandfather soldiered through both World Wars. His son, a teenage infanteer, fought at Tobruk, El Alamein, Kokoda and Borneo. My father left school and started full-time employment at 14. I'd had no intention of following in his footsteps, but I was 15 when I left school. For most people, though, those days are long gone.

A soldier aged in his late twenties who voluntarily removes himself from the course, whether or not he has personal issues clouding his mind, will not be afforded another chance. His dream will remain unfulfilled.

Some people are incapable of working alone. They require support, feedback, positive encouragement and camaraderie. The SAS requires team-oriented people who can also go it alone.

A few soldiers thrive on working independently. Skip, a fit man who won both the cross-country and triathlon races in the Regiment, gave me his thoughts on the solo navigation exercise at Lancelin in 1995. 'Mate, it was the best part of the course,' he said. 'Four days on your own with no one giving you shit – it was great!'

Skip was posted to the sniper troop, a job that requires plenty of patience and an ability to operate in the smallest of teams – two men. Skip's a solid operator and, despite having been dealt a few extra challenges in life, he's one of the mentally strongest and most balanced soldiers I've known. He's a tremendous asset to the Regiment.

I also enjoyed being left alone, but I definitely wouldn't go so far as to say stomping around Lancelin while being mauled by flies was great.

≡

Comfortable operating alone: Skip in Afghanistan.

On Tuesday 4 April, I arrived at my final checkpoint. I had completed approximately 68 kilometres. Some of the more experienced soldiers who really pushed themselves walked in excess of 80, while others completed less than 50.

I listened to a couple of guys from the 1st battalion explain how initially they'd tried to force their way through the dense three- to four-metre scrub. I was intrigued, because I'd spent the best part of four days burrowing through the shit. They'd done it once before using the ridgelines to skirt around the most inhospitable terrain. Other soldiers had used well-worn animal tracks. I was paranoid about using tracks and was conscious of my limitations, so I'd kept it simple and stuck to bearings and paces. Unlike some, I hadn't got lost − a couple of guys ended up outside the training area − but I had expended far more energy than I should have.

I could no longer feel the soles of my feet, and the tops of my shoulders were no better. I dug my nails into the skin on one shoulder but felt nothing. This numbness would remain for the next 10 or 12 weeks. My shins, knees, thighs and the backs of my hands were covered in hundreds of tiny thorns. I spent weeks squeezing little pieces of Lancelin out of my inflamed, tender skin.

I had no idea what to expect during the final five or six days of the course. This might in fact have been a good thing, because my naivety kept me sheltered. I would soon be in the ugliest place I had ever seen.

5

WEEK THREE: LUCKY DIP

Wednesday 5 April – day 15 – was another roping day. We received fresh rations for both lunch and dinner, a welcome change from the ration packs that only ever filled half the void.

That evening we were placed in squads of nine or 10 soldiers. At 2200, we commenced 'lucky dip', the final phase of the selection course. The next four and a half days would be the most physically demanding of my life.

A cool change swept across the landscape, and with it came rain. The DS could not have hoped for a more perfect end to the course. At 2230 our squad was placed in an ambush. After two and a half hours lying on our stomachs – the prone position – we were told to maintain a 50 per cent watch. Working in pairs, we could take turns sleeping but were not permitted to use sleeping bags.

I couldn't sleep. I had lost a lot of weight and shivered incessantly. In my diary I wrote: 'Coldest night ever'. I have since had many nights that have proven far more uncomfortable but, at the time, this night was my benchmark.

At 0445 we left the ambush location and patrolled to a

designated rendezvous (RV). It was a relief to get moving. Our packs, webbing and rifles kept us company, but we were also provided with a few other bits and pieces to drag along. First there were two trunks filled with sandbags, four metal poles and two lengths of rope. We lashed the poles to the trunks and headed towards our second RV, six kilometres away. Eight of us carried the two boxes while one guy walked ahead and navigated. A couple of men rotated through the navigational responsibilities; the rest struggled with the boxes.

The second activity was a four-kilometre stretcher carry, followed by a five-kilometre pack march. Our patrol was tasked to carry two 'casualties' – human-shaped dummies – to safety. An 80-kilogram man would have been a decent challenge, but these larger-than-life creatures were made from sandbags. While trying to raise the first stretcher, two of the squad members lost their balance, and the stretcher wedged into the back of one man's neck. He was then assigned light duties and instructed to walk ahead and navigate.

We tried again, our lower backs straining under the excessive weight. After considerable stuffing around, we were on our way. But we had walked less than 20 metres when the first stretcher went down. The DS then made a call for our patrol to ditch one of the stretchers. That was great, but it still didn't lighten our load. After another below-average effort, the DS removed a couple of sandbags.

'You guys are a joke. Seeing as this patrol has no heart, we'll remove the heart and lungs from your casualty; we might as well keep you all the same.'

Next they removed two sandbags from the centre of the

casualty. A little later they removed half of both of his legs. If my back wasn't about to snap, I would probably have found this overestimation of our combined ability a little amusing.

Our evening meal was identical to both breakfast and lunch. *Where's their imagination?* I thought. We were given nothing. That evening we were tasked to make a shelter large enough to accommodate our entire patrol. We had to continue working until the DS decided it was suitable.

We set about making a lean-to. By midnight our enthusiasm had begun to wane. It was obvious that this task was designed to keep us awake. Most of us had also had very little sleep, if any, the previous night. The DS hid in the bush and observed our actions. Who would continue to work, and who would walk into the darkness and lie down when they think no one is watching? My eyes were heavy. I felt delirious as I dragged my groundsheet covered with leaves to the shelter. I scattered them on top then went back to collect some more.

At 0130 we were ordered to establish a piquet and go to sleep. We were to be up by 0500, so each man had a 25-minute piquet to enjoy. I remember being woken for my turn. I sat up, glanced at my watch and spent the next 20 minutes fighting sleep. Surprisingly, at 0240 I felt awake and began to think about food. I drank some water, which helped to quieten my noisy stomach.

At 0245 I woke the next guy, got back into my sleeping bag, pulled my head deep inside and drifted off. With each change of shift I woke, checked my watch and became frustrated that I was awake. I heard others snoring – I craved some of that.

It was now 7 April – day 17. I couldn't believe I'd made it this far. But we still had three or four very long days to go. Breakfast was delicious – more of nothing. I didn't care, as the lack of sleep and food had left me feeling nauseated.

We struggled off to our next activity. *What a surprise*, I thought, *more stores to carry.* This time we were given four logs, two tyres, a box holding an engine, and several pieces of rope. We made a trailer that didn't roll. Every few metres, the wheels would flop to the sides and the trailer would grind to a halt. We persisted with this design throughout the morning.

At one point we heard the crack of a rifle shot. We took cover and waited. The noise had come from another patrol; one of the soldiers had accidentally fired his weapon – an unlawful discharge (UD). The offender had his rifle slung on his back, but the safety catch had disengaged on another piece of equipment. Some time later, when handling his weapon, his finger found the trigger – *bang!* This soldier completed the course but was not accepted.

He came back the following year, and the year after that. Anyone who trains for and completes three SAS selection courses is committed. He made it into the Regiment and has proven to be an outstanding soldier. Everyone fucks up or comes up short every now and then. I didn't have long to wait before it would be my turn.

We eventually decided to disassemble the trailer and carry the stores. I noticed that the sun was high. *On a normal day, it would nearly be lunchtime*, I thought. I began to see black spots, and my vision blurred and then narrowed. I stumbled a couple of times but kept going.

'Have you been drinking enough water?' asked the supervising DS.

'Yes, sir,' I replied. No sooner had those words escaped my mouth than the black spots returned. I stumbled again.

The DS stopped the activity and made me sit down on a log. The others were ordered to continue.

'How much water have you consumed today?' he asked me.

'At least two litres, sir,' I replied. Then I dropped the water bottle I was holding – my hand was shaking uncontrollably. *What the hell is going on?* The DS told the others to wait and called one of the patrol members over. Thommo, who was performing well, was ordered to set up his radio and call in a medivac.

'I'm alright, sir,' I said and then my body seemed to shit itself – not literally, but my vision blurred and my extremities began to spasm. I was a mess.

An ambulance arrived and I was told to get in. I tried to argue but was told to shut up. I was taken back to camp and examined by a couple of medics. A hardarse DS, whom I had run beside on one of the pack marches, came over to see what was going on.

'What's up?'

'I'm fine, sir,' I said. 'Just got dizzy and fell over.'

The medics pricked my thumb and assessed my blood sugar level.

'It's three times below the minimum range,' said the medic. He looked a little like Keanu Reeves, just bigger and fitter.

'Yeah, he's hypoglycaemic,' said a sergeant medic. 'At this stage of the course, most of them would be. But he's pretty lean. Give him a shot of glycogen and get him back out there.'

'Righto,' said Keanu.

I would later be in the same troop as Keanu. At the time he was working as a medic on the selection course to gain experience.

'How ya' doing, mate?' he said to me. 'When your blood sugar levels get that low the body just shuts down. I'll give you a shot of glycogen and you'll be on your way. Happy?'

'Yes, Corporal,' I said. I was relieved to not be thrown off the course.

My body had gone into glycogen debt, similar to what a marathon runner experiences when they 'hit the wall'. The body stores approximately 2000 kilocalories of glycogen. Endurance athletes – marathon runners, triathletes, cyclists and cross-country skiers – can delay the phenomenon by 'carbo-loading' the day before. We had not been afforded such a luxury.

I'd begun the course weighing in at 79 or 80 kilograms. Due to my age and the way I trained, I had a high metabolism and a low percentage of body fat. At the end of selection, I weighed in at 66 kilograms – a drop of 13 kilograms in less than three weeks. I don't know how he managed it, but there was a guy who began the course at 65 kilograms and hobbled off at the end looking like he had been released from a prisoner-of-war camp. Men aged in their mid to late twenties, especially those who had a slightly higher percentage of body fat, fared far better during the latter stages of the course. They may have found the first week taxing, but after that they maintained superior levels of endurance.

I had never felt like a weak prick before and I hated it. After the course I was told to get in the gym and work on my endurance levels. I didn't have to be told twice, and by the time I completed the post-selection reinforcement cycle, I had achieved a better balance between strength and fitness. I never wanted to feel physically vulnerable again.

≡

After being issued the glycogen injection, I was monitored for 60 minutes before being returned to my patrol. The men were seated in pairs, resting. Our next task was to pull and push a trailer filled with equipment up a dirt track, over a crest and beyond.

That evening our patrol was directed to move to a track/creek junction and RV with an agent. We would receive further directions upon arrival.

The agent, an SAS soldier, spoke with a ridiculous accent. It was hard to take him seriously, but when he said: 'Move to the hotbox and share the food amongst yourselves,' he could have been speaking Swahili and we would have understood. We removed the lid and shone a torch inside. Our first meal in two days was fish heads and rice soup. Those who could not bring themselves to eat it would not have the energy to complete the course. There wasn't a lot, but we divided what was on offer and devoured the lot.

The eighth of April, my birthday, was a day of dreams. The previous evening's meal had excited my stomach. I wanted more but had to be content to taste only my thoughts. I didn't think about sex, only food. *Chips and gravy, a slice of pizza . . . I'd even settle for a piece of bread smothered in margarine*, I thought.

Throughout the morning we had to carry a four-metre inflatable boat along a track. Those with previous roping experience, like the commandos, who had completed climbing and roping courses, were invaluable when it came to tying down the equipment. I knew a few basic knots – a round-turn-two-and-a-half-hitch and a reef knot – but as the saying goes, 'if you don't know knots, tie lots'.

I was placed in charge of our next activity. The Regimental Sergeant Major (RSM) delivered my instructions with a calm, no-nonsense demeanour. This man, aged in his forties, had finished the Regimental cross-country race that year in the top five. And he was always in the gym with a few of his mates, lifting big weights and screaming for just one more rep. His chunky forearms commanded respect. Like a key in a lock, he was a good fit for the position of RSM.

With the assistance of a commando reservist who was particularly adept at tying a 'truckie's knot', we fastened a rope to two trees on opposite banks of a deep creek. Then, using karabiners, we attached the boat to the rope and pulled it, laden with all of our packs, across the creek without allowing it to touch the ground. Our patrol, aided by a fallen tree, then traversed the gully. We completed the task with two minutes to spare.

We continued to another RV and were met by the man with the absurd accent from the night before. Once again, his accent annoyed me, but the last time we'd met he had given us food. This time he gave us two armoured personnel carrier (APC) tracks to carry. We rigged a single track to a pole. Four men carried each track, leaving one man spare to navigate. The same guy who had navigated several times previously volunteered himself again. This had become something of a habit – a frustrating one.

Traversing uneven ground made it difficult for us to spread the weight squarely. The taller men's spines were often ground into their pelvises as the shorties walked on their toes in an attempt to carry their share.

As my birthday drew to a close, I felt like shit but was pleased to have made it to the end of another day. There was no cake, or any food at all, for that matter. Day 18 was dead.

According to one of the DS who we spoke with after the course, on day 19 we were supposed to have been given a ration pack. But they forgot, so we filled our stomachs with water. Besides faecal matter, there is very little that I would not have eaten at this point. We were, literally, starving.

Once again, we were afforded little sleep. The following morning, we were given 13 jerry cans filled with water to carry between nine people. We each squeezed a jerry into our packs and then took turns carrying the remaining four. After a couple of hundred metres I felt like my forearms were going to explode. We soon changed tactics and slid a stick through the handle so we could carry one of the spares between two men. The DS in charge of this activity appeared genuinely concerned about the wellbeing of our patrol. After one short rest, I fell over while trying to stand up. *Not again*, I thought. The DS told me to take my jerry can out of my pack. I refused.

'Look, sir, if I can't carry my own pack then I shouldn't be here.'

'Alright, but if you fall over again I'm getting you out of here so the doc can have a look at you.'

I was certain that if this happened I would be forcibly removed from the course.

I tried to stay focused, counting my steps as I walked. Two other men fell over. I didn't want to sit down during rest stops, because trying to stand up was a greater effort than plodding along. We reached a dam. The DS told us to sit down and wait. He then walked off. The weather was changing and rain looked imminent.

At the edge of the dam was another pile of stores: 44-gallon drums, poles and more rope. We had to get ourselves, our personal equipment and the stores to the other side. Essentially, we were required to make a raft. The raft wasn't pretty but it held together.

We ferried half the guys and half the stores across to the other side. We swam beside or behind the raft, using our legs for propulsion. Two of us were tasked to swim the raft back to pick up the others. The water was freezing. I was probably in the water for 40 or 50 minutes, and I knew I had to change out of my wet clothes at the first available opportunity.

Still carrying our packs loaded with a single jerry can each, we walked for another 2.5 kilometres. With each step the water squelched from our boots. At our next rest stop I put on a clean and dry set of fatigues. I've usually got pretty solid legs, but as I dropped my pants I was shocked by the white sticks that appeared – they seemed half the size they had once been. I could easily cup my hands around my upper thigh and overlap my thumbs completely.

Our next task was to winch a three-tonne vehicle onto

the road using a series of pulleys. After we achieved this we were told to push it. One of the guys had injured his leg so he was ordered to steer. The remainder of the team pushed the vehicle for just over two kilometres. On one small rise, the vehicle stopped and began rolling backwards. We chocked the wheels with stones and then rolled the vehicle to and fro as we painstakingly ascended the positive gradient. The DS assisted us to push the vehicle over the crest, and we continued down the hill. It began to drizzle. We were physically shattered.

A cold snap arrived, and with it came heavy rain. The chill bit deep into our wet bodies. I tried to stop shivering as it made my muscles ache. In the early evening we met up with another patrol before being left to our own devices. In pairs, we joined our hootchies together and got into our damp sleeping bags. *Fuck me . . . this is ridiculous*, I thought.

We were soon told to dismantle our hootchies and move to a designated ambush position. Half the remaining patrols were placed in the same ambush. Throughout the night it rained, sometimes hard, sometimes soft, but it was always wet and always cold. At that point I didn't care if I was accepted into the SAS. I was spent. My body was struggling to regulate its temperature. My hunger was gone, replaced by shivering nausea.

In the early hours of 10 April 1995, I heard two voices, then some shooting. The ambush was sprung. Our patrol, as per our orders, assembled at the rear of the ambush location and departed. Over the next hour, the dark sky dissolved to grey and the rain stopped.

For the entire course I had taken each day as it came. I'd tried not to anticipate what lay ahead. But I was no longer able to do that. I pictured the instruction handbook we'd been given before we started the selection course. The dates written on the front page were 23 March to 10 April. It was now 10 April. Was this just another mind game, or would it indeed be over soon? In four and a half days we'd been given one meal – fish-head soup. We needed sustenance. If this was to be the last day, what time would it end? There might still be 17 or 18 hours to go.

We walked up a hill to a hangar and saw other groups of dishevelled men sitting inside it. Then I saw Rog's face. He too had lost a lot of weight, perhaps more than me.

'It's over, mate,' he said. 'We did it. We finished the fucking thing.'

Our feeble hands embraced in a solid shake. I dumped my pack and sat on the floor.

'You want a brew?' Rog asked.

'What – are we allowed?'

'Yeah, look over there.'

I sat down and removed my boot to inspect my foot and ankle. The strapping tape was cutting deep into my instep. It took me 10 minutes to tear it off, revealing a deep wound on top of my foot. The stench made me grimace. The skin on my foot was an ugly white and mushy, like a corpse pulled from the water. I looked up and saw the SI, the man who had orchestrated the three weeks of pain we'd endured, watching me. His face remained deadpan. Then he walked away.

You don't have to accept me, I thought, *but I've finished your course and I gave it everything I had. Neither you nor anyone else can ever take that away from me.*

Then came breakfast. Neatly arranged on several folding

tables were a dozen loaves of bread, buns, boxes of cereal, and milk. No hot food or anything too rich, as our stomachs wouldn't have handled it. I grabbed a hot cross bun and half-filled my cups canteen – my metal mug – with cocoa flakes and milk. I took a bite from the bun and dry-retched. I didn't even give myself a chance to swallow the brine before I took another bite and forced it down. It stuck in my oesophagus, then I began to hiccup. I drank some milk, which relieved the congestion, and I switched to cereal. Halfway through that, I finished the bun. I had eaten very little yet my stomach felt full and tight.

One soldier pulled up his shirt and said: 'Hey, check this out. I've got abs! I've never had abs before – they're usually covered with padding.'

I laughed to myself. *I've dropped so much weight that the ridges in my stomach are probably my backbone.*

We were permitted to shower, so I retrieved my toiletries and a towel from my echelon bag, threw on a pair of thongs and walked to the shower block. The place was abuzz with dirty, gaunt faces and bodies that carried the same weeping red sores, a legacy of one's pack or webbing rubbing through the skin.

Some guys were taking the piss out of each other, shocked by the change in their mates' faces and physiques. I set my shaving gear up on the sink and wiped the misty mirror. I hadn't seen my reflection for a couple of weeks. My eyes were sunken and dark, my cheeks dissolved flat. I was surprised just how tiny my head had become. It was as if my face had fallen off.

The sinews in my neck were more pronounced, and my clavicles were exposed like a shirtless coathanger. I could clearly see where my sternum connected to my rib cage. All this in less than three weeks.

Yet what we had endured was nothing in comparison to generations past. Millions of men and women – both allies and adversaries – suffered for years in POW camps. Of the 91,000 members of the German Sixth Army who surrendered at Stalingrad in World War II, only 5000 made it home. The majority perished in Soviet labour camps from disease and malnutrition.

≡

Having a crack at the SAS selection course was good for me. Sure, my aim was to become an SAS soldier, but being pushed beyond my limits taught me a lot about myself. As a person I had grown considerably, and over the next 12 months there would be much more to come.

I'd learnt many lessons, the most important being that if I wanted something badly enough, then I should trust myself and go for it. Life is full of pessimists, people who say something can't be done. And even if they're right and you fail – so what? Those who embrace their dreams and come up short have not truly failed. Failure belongs to those who didn't have the courage to step over the starting line.

≡

About thirty men remained, a mix of soldiers and officers. We boarded a coach and drove to Campbell Barracks, Swanbourne – the home of the Australian Special Air Service Regiment. I dozed most of the way, but the winged dagger on the front gates grabbed my attention.

Our first task was to clean our rifles. The quartermaster was stringent – he wanted them handed in spotless. I think we were given hotboxes for lunch, to control how much food we were eating. Our eyes were definitely larger than our shrunken stomachs. Going too hard too quickly could make us sick. For the rest of that afternoon we cleaned and returned our personal stores. There was a lot of sitting around.

While this was taking place, the DS were discussing the performance of each trainee in detail. Our test results, our leadership potential, our ability to work independently and as a member of a team, our capacity to absorb information, our personality, work ethic, integrity, discipline, physical fitness and endurance – all aspects were scrutinised by the panel.

As the hours passed our sense of anticipation grew. Everyone who remained had finished the selection course, but who would actually be selected?

Later that afternoon we were advised that the mess opened at 1700. Our next timing was 0730 the following morning, so our time until then was our own. We were escorted to the transit accommodation and issued rooms, four men to each one.

I went for a walk and found a payphone outside the Regimental Aid Post (RAP). I called Colleen and left a short message on her answering machine. I then called my parents and spoke with my mother. She was aware that I was doing some type of selection course, but she didn't really know anything much about the SAS. We were close and spoke often, sometimes for hours, but I had never explained the course in great detail, just in case I failed.

I told her I was pleased to have finished, and that if they didn't accept me I would try again the following year. Ma wished me luck and said she had a feeling I'd be accepted. Mother's intuition – if anyone knew what sort of person I was, it was her.

There were several guys waiting to use the phone so we didn't speak for long. Besides, it was nearly dinnertime and I wanted to see how much food I could squash into my stomach. Although I was full within five minutes, I kept eating for at least 30. My stomach ached and I found it difficult to breathe. I lay on my bed shirtless, my pants undone and my legs splayed, in an attempt to minimise any pressure on my stomach.

Rog stuck his head in my room. 'Hey, mate, a few of the guys are going to Fremantle to grab a beer and a steak. You coming?'

I felt like I was in labour and four weeks overdue. 'Nah, mate, I'm gonna chill out and lie here for a while.'

'Cool, brother, I'll see you tomorrow.'

Grab a steak? Are they freaking serious? I thought. *Just breathing hurts.* As it turned out, the guys didn't have the energy to party and were all in bed by 2300 that night.

I had a restless night's sleep and woke up hungry. I went to the mess and had a couple of bowls of chocolate cocoa flakes. I had just completed the most challenging course in the Australian military, yet when given the opportunity to eat, I chose a children's breakfast cereal ahead of pancakes, bacon, eggs and toast.

Just walking around still left me light-headed. I couldn't feel the soles of my feet at all, and after breakfast I spent 15 minutes squeezing thorns out of my shins, knees and thighs. The hours crawled by. We cleaned vehicles and anything else the quartermaster could think of. In the early afternoon, while we were seated on the grass outside the quartermaster's store, the SI made an announcement.

'The following men are to follow me inside. Everyone else is to remain in place.'

The SI disappeared with about eight men, a combination of soldiers and officers. When he returned we were told that those who remained had been found suitable for further training. There were no congratulations − just a warning that anyone who failed to perform during the next phase of the training would also be sent back to their units.

Colleen was right − we would be moving to Perth.

6

ACCEPTANCE VIA PERFORMANCE

I had passed the course and was accepted into the SAS. I was fortunate – not everyone in life realises what they want to do for a job and then sees it come to fruition. I had set a mid-term goal and had dedicated myself whole-heartedly to making it happen. Injury, age, endurance and negative comments were some of the obstacles I was confronted with, but from the outset I had known what I wanted and my motivation had not wavered.

Whenever I set myself big challenges, the first thing I do is ask: why am I doing this? What is my motivation? Without a strong and true desire, you'll struggle to push through adversity.

I wanted to work with the best soldiers in the Australian military, and I wanted to be deployed on the most challeng-ing tasks. I craved an exciting occupation where I would be tested. Soldiers don't join the SAS for money or because it sounds cool. The men are passionate about soldiering and strive to take it to the highest level. Desire spawns motiva-tion, and motivation creates opportunity. You don't need to venture far for that – motivation comes from within.

≡

The day after the selection course ended, we were granted four days' leave. The only proviso was that we must not do any physical training. For once in my life, going for a run or to the gym was the furthest thing from my mind. We were given some learning booklets to study at our own pace, but besides that our time was our own.

I was the only soldier from the 6th Battalion to pass the course, so initially I wasn't part of any clique. The guys from the other battalions, especially the 1st, 2nd and 3rd Battalions, were already tight.

Still feeling fatigued, I decided to walk to the beach to check out the ocean. I love the water and usually feel a sense of calm when in its presence. It was a cold, wintry day, and a strong southerly wind was sweeping up the coast. Campbell Barracks backs onto the Indian Ocean, a pristine and much sought-after location in the heart of Perth's 'golden triangle'. From the back gate of the barracks I followed an obvious sand track to a sentry tower that over-looked the beach. I climbed the tower, and while I was there an effeminate Asian man joined me. I thought this was a little weird, so I left.

I tucked myself into the northern side of a sand dune and watched the choppy waves slap against the sand while I drifted in and out of sleep. Fifteen minutes later, I opened my eyes and saw a man walking across the beach in front of me. He was staring at me intently. After a while he retraced his footsteps, walked around the sand dune I was sheltering behind and positioned himself 10 metres behind me. I immediately sat up and my body prepared itself for battle.

Surely this fucker isn't going to try and mug me, I thought. *Does he seriously want to have a go?*

I casually glanced over my right shoulder and eyeballed the man. With a furrowed brow, I turned my head back, stared at the sand in front of me and tried to work out if what I had just seen was real. *Did he just have his cock in his hand?* I looked at the man again, and this time there was no mistake – he was stroking his erect penis while staring at me.

'What in the hell are you doing?' I yelled.

The man, aged in his mid to late thirties, didn't say a word but tried to bend his cock back into his tracksuit pants. I stood up. He began to panic, trying to decide whether he should run or remain where he was.

I shouted: 'Are you fucking serious?' and kicked some sand towards him. Before me was a man who was uncomfortable with confrontation. He rolled onto his side and crumpled onto the sand.

I had no intention of taking it any further. I stormed up the beach and didn't look back. I told a few of the guys what had happened, and for a short time I was nicknamed 'Dune Boy'. It was then I learnt that Swanbourne Beach was a hangout for gay men. I should have realised that when the other guy had joined me in the sentry tower.

My issue was not that the man was homosexual – people's sexual preference has never bothered me. He has as much control over choosing his sexuality as I do: none. But I found his actions confronting as they caught me off guard. It was the same as if a heterosexual male had been tossing off while looking at a woman on a beach.

In fact, the first guy I told was homosexual. He had also passed the selection course and would become a close mate of mine. When he saw my reaction, he told me much later, his initial thoughts were: *Great, Fenno's homophobic. There's no way I'll ever be able to be honest with this guy.*

He was wrong. I found out about his sexual preference two years before he came out publicly, and I kept it a close secret. I always considered him to be an exceptional soldier and often commented to my wife that he was one of the most grounded and mentally secure soldiers I knew.

Some people have a perception – created by the aggressive nature of SAS training and operations – that all SAS soldiers are Alpha males. But it's only partly true. Most of the guys are complex individuals, and are far more open-minded about things that fall outside the 'norms of society' than most people expect. When bullets are slamming into the earth around you – when things become a little crazy – there are no thoughts or concerns about anyone's sexuality. Why should there be? All you give a fuck about is whether the guy next to you is competent, and whether he'll stay by your side if the situation becomes dire.

My first days in the Regiment were definitely interesting. But there was much more to come.

=

The next night, the majority of the soldiers on our reinforcement cycle went to the Swanbourne Hotel for a few drinks. A couple of men tried to position themselves above others – an alcohol-induced, self-proclaimed order of seniority. Considering I had only joined the military the previous year, they felt they had to let me know that I was a 'jube' – a new guy – and so relegated to the bottom of their pecking order. I was advised to keep my mouth shut and learn. I wasn't the only guy who was spoken to that night. Initially, there was a dominant group within our cycle. It's easy to govern as a pack, especially when you're targeting lone guys who are yet to establish themselves.

An officer also chimed in, having a crack at me for being a 'Ready Reserve' soldier. 'I heard you were a Ready Red Rooster,' he said at the top of his voice. He repeated this several times, laughing out loud and then he began to crow.

I just nodded my head and smiled. I looked at the man and thought: *You look more like a goose than a rooster.* I remained reserved and eventually returned to the barracks. It's not a long walk – 1.2 kilometres at most – along a road lined with pine trees. But it was long enough for me to reflect on what was said.

At first I tried to recall if I had said something to antagonise these guys. *Was I being a smartarse?* But then I wondered to myself why guys like them waited so long before attempting selection. If they were so good, why did it take them so many years to make it into the Regiment? Was it a lack of confidence? Did they need to wait for a dozen of their mates to do it with them? Sure, some of them had big reputations in the Battalion, but we weren't in the Battalion anymore. We would all have a steep learning curve, but mine would be a little steeper.

I'd made it into the SAS but I felt like an outsider. The last time I felt this way was 18 years earlier, at pre-school. I still remember a red-headed girl and three boys banishing me from the tree-house because I was wearing a belt.

Photo time at pre-school, aged four.

For weeks the group followed me around and hounded me off every piece of equipment in the playground. I began to hate Tuesdays – pre-school day – so I conned Ma into letting me stay at home. As a four-year-old I was shy and lacked confidence, but this was no longer the case.

Sitting on my bed, I mulled over a couple of options: I could confront those responsible and have it out, or I could double my efforts and earn their respect via performance. I was already highly motivated, but their comments did inspire me to work a little harder.

The next day, while the others recovered from their hangovers, I spent hours working with a piece of rope, practising my knots. Our first course was a four-day roping course.

I also began to familiarise myself with Morse code. We would later be expected to send and receive Morse at 10 words per minute. After memorising the characters, I began to practise on my Morse trainer – a device that beeped random characters, both letters and numbers. There were dials to control the sound and speed.

I'd wake up early, throw on a set of headphones and practise while the others slept. This continued throughout the day. Whenever I had a few spare minutes, I'd turn on my Morse trainer and scribble the characters into a large notebook. When it was full, I bought another.

Before our signals course even began, I could comfortably watch television and receive Morse at over 14 words per minute. I was tested at the end of the first week of the course and was the first to qualify.

During our survival training we were given a lesson on lock-picking. That evening, with Chris, a diligent, intelligent soldier who had a keen interest in demolitions, I purchased some hacksaw blades and we set about crafting our own set of lock picks. Each evening while watching television, I would work my way through a dozen padlocks. When I became bored with this I used to break into Todd's room, or wander outside and pick the ignition lock of a mate's Toyota 4Runner.

After our reinforcement training, I returned home and went to visit my father at his workshop. His front door is stitched with deadlocks, sliding bolts and padlocks. I pulled a lock pick and torsion bar out of my wallet and began raking the pins.

Dad scoffed and said: 'You'll never get through those.'

Five minutes later I opened the door and shot my father a grin.

'Jesus,' he said. 'I'll have to get another couple of padlocks.'

I laughed, relocked the door and tried again. My next attempt was quicker.

The men who had a go at me at the beginning of the reinforcement cycle were, in fact, excellent soldiers and decent guys. They'd been drinking that night and shot their mouths off. There probably isn't a person alive who, under the influence of alcohol, hasn't done this – me included. But I was young and took their comments to heart. I have always possessed an extreme desire to perform, their comments only made me more obsessive.

By the time we reached our dive course, two months into the reinforcement cycle, we were aware not only of how we were performing, but also of how everyone else stacked up. Past reputations now meant nothing. Those who worked hard did well. Those who didn't, or who perhaps were not suited to special operations, struggled or were moved on. Strong friendships were forged, and by the end of our reinforcement cycle many of us were inseparable.

I would later work with one of these guys for years, both in the Regiment and when contracting in Iraq and Afghanistan. I've always admired his toughness and the satirical, almost cavalier manner in which he negotiates dangerous situations. Ten years after our selection course he still remembered what he'd said.

'Mate,' he told me, 'I know I've said it before, but I just want to apologise for giving you shit at the Swanny that night. Bloody hell – of all the guys to have a crack at!'

I laughed. 'Yeah, don't worry about it. We were young and you were full of piss.'

'No excuse. I was a prick. It's always bothered me, mate, and I just wanted to let you know.'

'You do know you did me a favour? You guys inspired me to go harder.'

'Bullshit! You would have gone hard anyway.'

This guy later sent me an inspiring email after reading

Warrior Brothers. He didn't have to, but he took the time to craft something special. I realised then that we can all be hypercritical beasts at times, but those who grow the most are those who reflect with the deepest honesty.

≡

SAS soldiers are selected for their ability to think clearly during high-stress situations. This sometimes means suppressing your natural survival instincts. The comprehensive training SAS soldiers receive, coupled with mental preparation – mentally rehearsing the sequence of actions that are to be carried out – allows them to make the right decision in a timely manner. This training once saved my life.

We were on a parachute training exercise. As we all fitted our parachutes – pulling down on the leg straps, wiggling our hips and making grunting noises – an outsider would have thought we were engaged in some kind of torturous bonding ritual. You then have to bend over and heave on your shoulder straps. As you attempt to stand up it feels like your neck and genitals have been squashed into your stomach.

If a rogue testicle isn't tucked away properly, it is now that a man will pay the price: the straps will tear into his groin without remorse. It's easy to tell if a man has been a little careless when packing himself away, because a leg strap biting into a testicle is not something a man can hide. His face will contort, and a web of veins in his face and neck will pulse to the surface. This is usually followed by a squeal that would embarrass a kitten as he bends over again, his fingers frantically trying to free himself. SAS soldiers are a passionate lot; besides laughing, they may well come to their mate's aid and further tighten his shoulder straps.

Standing semi-hunched while waiting for parachute safety checks is as much fun as walking barefoot across a lawn full of bindies. I ogled the safety supervisor who was methodically working his way down the line, wondering why he was taking so long. I then noticed that he too was squashed into a parachute harness, and that his face had taken on the same hue as an overripe tomato.

He arrived — grinning — and began tugging at my equipment. 'Hey, Fenno, your static line looks dodgy. I'd use another parachute if I was you.'

'You freefall pussies are such pessimists,' I replied. 'It's only 1000 feet and we're landing in water — we probably don't even need a parachute.'

We were conducting an 'over the horizon' night jump, and the wind was gusting at 20 to 25 knots, the maximum allowable speed when jumping into water. Although we were jumping 'roundies', with a 50-kilogram pack hanging off the front of our harnesses, we had no fears about breaking a leg or shortening our spines, since we were only jumping into water.

Our Squadron Sergeant Major bellowed at us: 'Zulu One, winds are on limits but we'll make the decision whether or not you jump once we're over the drop zone. Move to the aircraft!'

We grabbed our packs and waddled out the hangar door towards the C130 aircraft, relieved that we would soon be in the water and able to take a piss. Once aboard, no one switches off. We fitted our seatbelts and silently recited the order in which things will take place. *The sooner we exit this claustrophobic, gut-wrenching machine, the better*, I thought.

'Six minutes,' the safety supervisor shouted, and we repeated his call down the line.

We stood up, hung our packs off the front of our harnesses, and then attached our parachute static lines to the cable overhead. The faint red glow illuminating the cabin was soon interrupted by another safety supervisor, who moved down the line with a flashlight, blinding the boys as he carried out his final safety checks. All joviality was now gone, and the men had moved into their own private worlds of deep concentration. The safety supervisor remained professional and offered little more than a wink and reassuring slap on the shoulder to confirm that my checks were complete.

With the rear ramp down, the three-minute call was silenced as the wind lashed the rear of the aircraft. The 30-second call saw us shuffle into position, bunched tight, adrenaline coursing through our bodies. All the men were wearing their fins – flippers – to negate any additional hassle when we hit the water. The only possible drawback, besides catching the wind as we exit the aircraft and being flipped upside down, would be a slightly delayed departure. We were to follow our two Zodiacs – four-metre black boats powered by twin 25-horsepower engines – out of the aircraft, and for every additional second we wait before jumping, we can expect a 100-metre swim. A four-second delay equates to a good 400 metres. We waited, staring at the red light and willing it to turn green.

The green light kickstarted our hearts and our boats punched into the night, their large parachutes springing to

Parachuting into Singapore Harbour.

life. We attempted to drive hard off the ramp, but with the hindrance of our fins we could only dribble out the back like penguins, falling head first and off balance. My fins caught the wind and I flipped over onto my back. My sweaty hands remained white-knuckled across my reserve chute, ready to deploy it should it be required.

My chute opened with a violent jolt. *My testicles may well be squashed*, I thought, *but there's no time to ponder such trivialities*. It was time to unlock my toggles and steer towards the boats, which themselves would soon be in the water. Fixated on the closest craft, I willed myself across the black sky. Thirty feet above the water, I undid my chest-snap – the clip that secured the top of my harness – and unclipped my left capewell – a metal tab – to expose the small wire ring that, when pulled, would collapse one side of my parachute.

I assessed my speed and noticed that I was flying backwards. The water reflected just enough light to show me that I was going to land hard. I began to breathe quickly, trying to time my last breath before I made contact. The black water was flying under my feet like a treadmill on full speed.

I slammed into the water, and the gentle sound of the wind was overwhelmed by the gushing waves that filled my ears. I exhaled through my nose and mouth as I tugged at my left capewell, attempting to collapse the parachute, but the fucker would not release – it had seized up, perhaps because of one too many saltwater jumps. The wind gusted hard and I was dragged underwater, the parachute now acting as a kite.

My pack was still attached to my stomach, as I hadn't bothered to lower the line – it was just another thing to get tangled in the water. My heart was sprinting and my lungs were begging for air. With a greater level of commitment and using both hands, I wrenched on my capewell again, but still it refused to release.

I was caught in an ugly place. My instincts were to claw at the surface and attempt to get my head above water, but my training – a voice that was beginning to fade – told me to settle the fuck down and to try my other capewell. I reached to my right shoulder to locate the coin-like tab at the apex, but the cold water was inhibiting my dexterity. I felt like a beetle trapped on its back.

My body was pulled taut as the wind screamed again. To conserve my energy, I had to resist the urge to kick and thrash my way towards the surface. Finally, I located my right capewell, released the tab, put my thumb through the ring and pulled hard. *If only masturbation was this exciting.* I was still underwater, but my speed appeared finally to be slowing. My head broke the surface, I gasped for air and my chute collapsed into the water.

After half a dozen salt-watery coughs, I removed my leg snaps, pack, belly band and lowering line. I pushed myself up onto my pack and did a quick 360, expecting to see a safety craft so I could offload my parachute and get going. But as I rose and fell across the swells, all I could see was dark, choppy water. There was no sign of the red Cyalume glowsticks that should be illuminating the boats.

Although I was supposed to hand the apex of my parachute to a safety craft, I had no intention of wrestling with it in the dark. The harness, which I was holding in my left hand, would have to do. I removed a green Cyalume from my right wetsuit sleeve, cracked it and waved it above my head. I did another 360-degree turn but met with only cold, eerie darkness. I was 20 nautical miles off the West Australian coast, and unpleasant thoughts of what might be lurking beneath me briefly entered my mind, but there was little point worrying about the outcome of what would have been a brief and one-sided encounter.

After another 20 minutes passed, I saw the glow of a safety craft some 200 metres away. Again I waved the Cyalume above my head, before placing it in my mouth so I could kick more firmly to keep my head above water. I held onto my pack with my right hand, only letting go every now and then to wave the Cyalume towards the safety craft. My parachute had submerged completely, and remaining afloat required a sustained effort. I was no longer bobbing above the swells but was dragged through them by my heavy parachute.

After 35 minutes in the water I was struggling to stay afloat. I considered ditching my parachute but decided that drowning would probably be less embarrassing. *I'll reassess after 45 minutes*, I thought. Finally, after about 40 minutes, a safety craft meandered over. I passed my parachute harness to the bowman.

'Hey, mate,' he said. 'Both your boats are upside down – the closest one is probably 300 metres that way. If you have trouble finding it just give us a wave. We've still got one more guy to account for.'

I selected a star on the horizon as a point of reference and set off, relieved to be free of my parachute. I reached the boat 10 minutes later. It had been flipped upside down and its engines were full of water. As we worked on the engines in the dark – removing the spark plugs and pulling the engines over – the heavy seas and sickly waft of fuel saw all of us share the contents of our stomachs with the ocean. Twenty minutes later we were ready to go.

'Hey, guys,' yelled a man from the safety craft. 'The wind's picked up, so the exercise has been cancelled.'

Damn! Those fucking freefallers miss out again, I thought. I pictured them taking their parachutes off and laughing as they got back on the bus. Although I knew we still had a two-hour kidney-thumping transit to go, it was nights like this that attracted me to the Regiment.

While being dragged backwards underwater, my instinct had been to thrash around in order to get my head above water. But because of the severity of the wind gusts, this would have been futile. Remaining flexible does not mean cuffing it when things go wrong. If you have a plan, then it's more efficient to modify that plan than to formulate a new solution from scratch. My training, not my instincts, helped me to make the right decisions under testing conditions.

≡

The men who passed the selection, roping, patrol and basic parachute courses returned to their units for four weeks, where each was to organise his removal and collect his belongings. I went back to Brisbane but was sent straight out to the bush, to play enemy for the new platoons that were completing their infantry employment training (IET).

My first task was to move to the junction of a road and a creek, wait for it to get dark and then ambush an infantry section. A couple of hours after last light, my colleague and I saw a distant glow through the vegetation. When the glow began to flicker and move, it became obvious it was a torch.

'You reckon those guys are looking for this junction?' asked my colleague.

'Yeah, probably,' I replied.

'Why would they be walking through the bush with a torch?'

'Don't know . . . maybe they're lost,' I said.

We didn't have to wait long to find out. Out of the dark screamed a voice: 'Enemy . . . enemy . . . where are you?'

I recognised the voice immediately. It belonged to the tool who had questioned my navigational experience a couple of months earlier. We remained quiet.

'Is this guy for real? He's walking around with a torch?' said my colleague.

I moved onto the road and watched the torchlight disappear into the bush some 150 metres away, amid his fading screams of desperation: 'Enemy . . . enemy . . .'

We decided to remain in our ambush location. Ten minutes later we heard footsteps running up the track. They stopped 50 metres shy of our position and the familiar yells continued: 'Enemy . . . enemy . . . is anyone there?'

We remained quiet and the footsteps scurried away. Fifteen minutes later he was back. The lone man stopped across from our position, bent over and sucked in some large breaths. I thought about initiating the ambush and brassing him up. 'Enemy!' he screamed again.

'We're over here,' I replied.

'Thank fuck for that! Man, that's tiger country. We hit the wrong junction,' said the man, shining his torch in our direction.

How much nav ya' done? I thought, as the man's torch beam found my smiling face. I could tell he remembered our previous conversation, so what more was there to say? We ambushed his section and that was that.

7

RTI TRAINING: A TEST
OF SELF-BELIEF

Resistance-to-interrogation training – more commonly
known to soldiers as 'RTI' or 'getting bagged' –
is a profound test of one's mental strength and
self-belief.

Our troop had spent several days on a field training
exercise. Our mission: to rescue the crew of a downed helicopter. With this completed, we boarded a couple of army
trucks to be extracted. Although we were aware that RTI
training was looming, the exact dates remained a secret so
as to maximise the 'shock of capture'. When all the new
guys were guided onto the same truck, we knew something was going down.

As our transport pulled into a brightly-lit hangar, it was
surrounded by dozens of men dressed in black and white
military fatigues. I gave them a smoke grenade to suck on
and 30 blank rounds, which I fired on full automatic
before a man with a pornstar moustache approached the
back of our truck and yelled: 'Time out, time out! Put
down your weapons and play the game. You have been
captured. This is RTI.'

Putting up a fight was pointless. We knew the RTI experience was a requirement that all SAS soldiers must endure. *Bring it on*, I thought.

The acronym 'RTI' sounds pleasant enough, rolling off the tongue a bit like NFI – no fucking idea – but for me those three letters, in that sequence, conjure up a range of memories, from aching knees and hypothermia to 'bend over and spread your buttocks'.

I knew RTI would last for 72 hours, the length of a long weekend. Most soldiers complete RTI during their reinforcement cycle – the first 12 months in the Regiment before being posted to an SAS sabre squadron – but in our case the training took place the following year, four months after we had joined a squadron.

The aim of RTI is to educate soldiers about what to expect and how to react should they ever be captured by an enemy. It also provides interrogators – selected personnel from the Royal Australian Intelligence Corps – with guinea pigs to practise on. I reckon it's reasonable to draw a parallel between interrogators and male gynaecologists; there are those who are professional and brilliant at what they do, and there are those who might more aptly be described as 'suspect individuals'.

For the training to be effective, a captive is firstly fatigued – worn down by sleep deprivation, a lack of sustenance and extreme physical activity. He'll also be stripped of his visual and aural senses – made to wear blacked-out goggles and earmuffs – to disorient him. The captives are then pitted individually against a well-drilled team of intelligence officers, whose sole aim, generally speaking, is to extract information.

During times of war, what a soldier says during his or her first 72 hours in captivity might well decide not only their own fate but also the fate of others who have eluded capture. Additionally, if he or she releases key information about a mission then they could easily jeopardise ongoing operations. Therefore, in accordance with the Geneva Convention, soldiers are instructed to provide only 'the big four' – name, rank, regimental number and date of birth – and 'nothing more'. Considering that it's obviously illegal to yank out teeth, sodomise a captive, remove digits or break bones during training, you could argue that RTI training is unrealistic; in the current climate, at least, our adversaries' preference has been for other, more violent interrogation techniques.

In reality, when soldiers are threatened with decapitation unless they read dodgy confessions, they'll instinctively say whatever is required to remain alive. Furthermore, with the release of the graphic images of Iraqi prisoners being mistreated in the Abu Ghraib prison, it's evident that even countries who are signatories to the convention have at times failed to adhere to its requirements. But irrespective of whether or not the 'big four' was realistic, I knew that, if name, rank, regimental number and date of birth was all the information we were permitted to give, then that's all the information these intelligence clowns were going to get from me.

Before going 'into the bag' I was, somewhat naively, looking forward to the experience. *Seventy-two hours*, I thought. *It's not like they're allowed to break my arms or have their way with me. How difficult can it be?*

'Hey, Fenno,' asked one of the boys. 'You reckon we'll get bagged on our next patrol?'

'Hope so,' I replied. 'I'm keen to see if it's as punishing as everyone makes out.'

'What – you *want* to do it?'

'Absolutely!'

'What the fuck for?'

'I'm curious – and I'm sick of listening to everyone who has done it gob off about how fucked it is. It's only 72 hours.'

≡

Seventy-two naked, humiliating, wintry hours gave me a far greater appreciation of time. Three days is a bloody long time when someone else is in control of your life. Besides motivating me to never allow myself to be captured, RTI taught me a lot about myself. During those days of isolation, being subjected to sleep deprivation and water-board treatment – being seated in a mud pool and blasted by a fire hydrant – interspersed with several interrogation sessions, I knew I had to back myself, regardless of what was going on around me.

Todd and I were the first two guys dragged from the truck. Standing at six foot three, Todd was a large and pretty aggressive young man. He was also one of the better soldiers in the troop. He probably wasn't a people person. In fact, Todd didn't like people very much, but he did like me and a few others. On Todd's buck's night, we dressed him up in a black lycra suit and a gimp mask. He was furious but we all thought it was hilarious. Towards the end of the night, Todd was walking down the main street of Subiaco with Stevie when they were bailed up by a couple of louts.

'Hey, check out the fucking faggot,' said one.

The big guy in the lycra suit responded by knocking him out.

I wondered how Todd, one of my best mates in the troop, would get along with our interrogators.

Within seconds our hands were cuffed behind our backs, blacked-out goggles were put over our faces and muffs were placed on our ears. I was then led away, pushed into a stress position and searched. I heard the muffled sounds of a dog – a German shepherd – close by, and I smelt its rancid breath. The dog began to bark and growl, its saliva slapping my right cheek. Then, perhaps getting a little too excited, it made a choking sound and its master whispered commands of restraint. This made me laugh.

Someone grabbed me by the hair, lifted up my left earmuff and said in a sinister tone: 'You will play the fucking game, arsehole.'

Considering my face reeked of dog saliva, I was less concerned about the profane language than I was about whether or not that foul-breathed dog was infested with worms. After some time – possibly an hour – I was led away, pushed into the back of a padded vehicle and driven around. The driver, who had a tendency to brake into corners, drove like my 82-year-old grandmother: fast and erratically. The vehicle stopped and I was grabbed by the hair, led across a gravel surface and into a building. Two guards escorted me down what seemed like a long hallway. We passed through several rooms and several doors. My head was pushed down, as if to create an impression that we were entering small rooms. Then we stopped, my earmuffs were removed and the guards walked away. For several minutes there was nothing. No shuffling of feet, no whispers, no sounds of breathing, nothing. I tried not to swallow and my ears were straining for sound.

Then a voice came out of nowhere: 'You are a prisoner of war and are not permitted to escape. Do you understand?'

'I cannot answer that question,' I replied.

'We will now remove your handcuffs,' said the voice.

I was somewhat relieved about this. My fingers were numb and the plastic cuffs had cut deep into my wrists.

The voice, serious and stern, continued: 'Remove your shirt and place it on the floor behind you.'

I followed the instructions.

'Remove your boots, socks and trousers and place them on the floor behind you.'

Once again, I followed the commands.

'Remove your underwear and place your hands on your head.'

I bent over, slid my underwear down my legs and took half a step forward with my left leg as I eased my underwear behind me with my right foot. I remained slightly hunched, my hands atop my head. For what felt like hours, but in reality might have been only a couple of minutes, I stood there in total silence, tense, exposed and vulnerable. Then the silence was broken.

'You will now be searched. Do not resist.'

My body was searched in a methodical manner by someone wearing rubber gloves: my hair, ears, the inside of my mouth, my armpits, groin and the soles of my feet. I thought – I hoped – it was over.

Then came the finale: 'Bend over and spread your buttocks.'

The person wearing the rubber gloves took his – or maybe her – time. Bent over and with my hands pulling my arse cheeks apart, I wondered if the army was legally allowed to stick a finger into my anus? I then heard slapping sounds as the gloves were stretched and released several times. That snapping sound of rubber on skin made my sphincter contract. A hand briefly touched my right buttock. My sphincter contracted more. I waited, still wondering if this was permissible in training. I swallowed a mouthful of saliva, which somehow made me feel better.

I then thought: *Fuck it*, and I zoned out. I let my mind go blank and became a zombie who didn't care. The gloves stretched and snapped several more times but the sounds were not sharp like they had been. They were distant and beyond offence. I was asked to relax my sphincter, which I did. Only a small piece of my mind remained open. I was able to follow simple commands but my emotions were not affected.

'Stand up,' said the voice.

Time to return to reality, I thought, and I switched back on, relieved that no attempt was made to fondle my prostate. I also realised that our interrogators had limitations – they were indeed not permitted to finger my arse.

'We will now remove your goggles,' the voice said. 'You are to look straight ahead. Do you understand?

'I cannot answer that question,' I replied.

'Don't try to be a tough guy. Do you understand?'

'I cannot answer that question.'

'A simple "yes" is all that is required. Do you understand?'

Once again, my reply was: 'I cannot answer that question.' This little game reminded me of the yes/no game my father played with my sisters and me when we were growing up. I had learnt then that the key is to pause after each question. Each question must be analysed separately from the ones before it. You cannot control the number or speed of the questions that are being asked, but you can control the pace of your answers. Regardless of how many questions the exasperated interrogator threw my way, I would take my time and answer the first one only. The interrogator's friend – momentum – is the captive's foe.

When my goggles were removed, the pain at the back of my eyes was like an extreme ice-cream headache. My eyes had no time to adjust, thrust from darkness into the most intense white lights I had ever seen.

'Look at me,' boomed the voice.

This guy thinks he's the Wizard of Oz, I thought. The numerous sharp glows that stabbed my eyes made it impossible to put a face to the voice. Through the light I could vaguely make out a desk, perhaps with someone seated behind it.

'What's your name?' said the voice.

'Keith Fennell.'

'Your full name?'

Prick, I thought. 'Keith Gerard Fennell,' I said.

'Spell it.'

I did.

'What's your rank?'

'Private,' I replied.

'From the equipment you were carrying it is evident that you are an SAS soldier. Therefore your rank would be trooper. What's your rank?'

'Private.'

'I'm going to ask you this question again. If you fail to tell the truth then you will not be protected by the Geneva Convention. Do you understand?'

'I cannot answer that question.'

This continued for several minutes, and the interrogator became increasingly agitated.

'What's your regimental number, Trooper Fennell?'

'I cannot answer that question.' The interrogator was addressing me as Trooper Fennell rather than Private Fennell, so I decided that I would not answer his question. I had to keep every question simple.

'You are obliged – you must answer that question!' yelled the voice. 'What's your regimental number, Fennell?'

I began to rethink my decision to declare my rank as private rather than trooper. Technically they are the same, but I decided there and then to continue with private, regardless of the repercussions.

The bright lights were turned off and the burning sensation at the back of my eyes dissolved. Before me, illuminated now by the regular room lighting, sat a bespectacled, pot-bellied man aged in his mid-fifties, with grey hair and a greyer beard. The voice now had a face.

After that glimpse, I decided to zone out again, staring at the top of the interrogator's head with lifeless, unfocused eyes. This seemed to annoy him, as he eventually left the safe confines of his desk and stood right in front of me, staring directly into my face. I could only presume that he was staring into my eyes but I kept my vision blurred so that his face resembled a grey hairy ball.

The interrogator asked the same questions over and over again. Occasionally I returned to the present and thought about how much I would like to knee him in the groin, but as his rants intensified and his spit splattered my face, I returned to the surreal comfort of emptiness.

'What's your rank?' said the angry grey hairy ball.

'Private,' I replied.

'What's your rank?'

'Pr –'

'Liar,' he interjected. 'What's your rank?'

'Private.'

'Liar. Your rank is trooper. What's your fucking rank?'

'Private.'

'Take this idiot away and let him have a think about it,' said the grey hairy ball.

My vision and hearing were once again stolen from me as the guards refitted my goggles and muffs. I was led out of the room, across a gravelled surface that pained my soft feet and into another building. The night air of the Northam winter chilled my skin, and over the next few hours this cold would seep into my core.

The guards pushed me onto the floor, crossed my legs and placed my hands on my knees. I would spend the best part of 48 hours in this position, the only respite coming in the form of punishment or sessions with the interrogators. For hours I sat there with aching knees, my arse numbed by the wooden floor. Although the goggles had a foam seal, they were painfully tight. With each hour they cut deeper into my face, until the pain across my forehead was on a par with my aching knees. Whenever I attempted to transfer weight from one arse cheek to another, a guard would grab my shoulders and force me onto the ground. The same would happen if a hand slipped from my knee.

I began to taunt the guards, letting one hand slide off my knee and then slowly replacing it as their footsteps approached. I heard other people coughing and realised I was not alone. I continued to amuse myself by sliding a hand off my knee and then returning it. *Nothing too obvious – just a couple of times an hour*, I thought. On one occasion I lowered my hand immediately after hearing the guard's footsteps fade. I then heard a floorboard behind me creak. *Fuck*, I thought, as an aggressive hand grabbed my hand and slapped it onto my lower thigh. The man pushed his knee into my back, raised my left muff and whispered into my ear: 'Don't do it again, arsehole.'

At one point I was dragged outside and pushed into a muddy pool of water, no more than a foot deep. But the gravelly bottom ground into my arse, and small stones wedged between my cheeks as well as my toes. Someone removed my muffs and told me that I was being punished because I lied about my rank. I sat there shivering, when suddenly a heavy blast of water smashed against my body. Compared to the deathly night air, the water actually felt warm. After a moment it stopped and the night air bit into my skin, and then the water came again.

I lowered my head, zoning out. I thought of

Resistance-to-interrogation training was a test of self-belief.

nothing – not the pebbles against my arse, not the metallic taste of the water or the cold against my skin. Nothing.

After half a dozen repetitions of this I was dragged from the pool and put inside a large freezer. Hanging out in a freezer after some quality time under a fire hydrant redefined my perceptions of what it was to be cold. I tried to mentally remove myself from that space in a feeble attempt to escape the cold, but I could not. I then thought about my grandfather and great-grandfather, and what they must have endured during the World Wars. Unfortunately, though, their stories are as dead as they are. No letters, no diaries – only pictures, medals and a few blurry memories remain.

I barely knew my grandfather or his father and yet, when tucked into the foetal position inside a freezer,

My grandfather Jack Fennell (second from right), after capturing a piece of German armour in the Middle East during World War II.

I thought of them. We were related, and their experiences gave me strength. I had been cold before – I knew what it was like to shiver – but this was special. At first I remained hunched over, nauseated and shaking just a little. But as time dragged on, the deep contractions within my muscles intensified, to the point where my body began to relax and ceased to tremble – the onset of hypothermia.

The day before my grandfather Jack died, I gave him a small ceramic pig I made in art class. Although Ma thought my creation was a hippopotamus, I was proud of that pig. I wondered where it was now. Then I visualised my interrogators' faces and thought: *Fuck 'em. Anyone who thinks up sick shit like this doesn't deserve to be told anything*. I don't imagine I was thinking too straight at this time, but I do remember being pulled from the freezer, taken to a room and given a blanket. *Hot or cold – I wish these fuckers would make up their minds*.

I was kept there until my core temperature rose. We later learned that the Regimental Medical Officer (RMO) was keeping a close eye on all of us during this phase of the exercise.

When Stevie, a hard-hitting operator with more attitude than a high-class hooker, collapsed onto the floor shaking, he was immediately removed from the training and examined by the doc.

'Steve, are you alright, mate?'

'Yeah, I'm just bunging it on,' he'd said.

'What, there's nothing wrong?'

'Nah, nothing – I'm good to go.'

'Guards, he's okay. Take him away.'

Stevie managed to surprise our interrogators on more than one occasion. In the middle of one heated session, he raised his hand and informed his interrogators that he needed to take a piss. He was told to hold on to it. Mr Attitude no doubt remained expressionless as he let go and pissed all over himself.

'Hey – what are you doing? Stop that, you fucking filthy man!' screamed the interrogators. Stevie ignored the abuse and continued to piss.

'If you want to act like a dog then we'll treat you like one,' one of them said. They had lost their momentum, and so, in an attempt to regain the upper hand, one of them grabbed Stevie by the hair and rolled him in his own urine.

=

I spent most of the next day seated cross-legged on a folded blanket. We were instructed to perform a range of activities, depending on the number of gongs we heard. This was both annoying and a relief, for my knees were aching constantly. I don't remember the sequence, but one gong might have meant stand up, two to jog on the spot, and three to sit back down. This annoying game continued for hours. The following evening I was taken once again to the mud pool, blasted by the fire hydrant and then chilled in the freezer. My next interrogation session, however, was a little different.

There were two interrogators, one male and one female. The man continued to question me about my rank, informing me that I was an idiot and too pathetic to be an SAS soldier.

'Look at you, standing there, your shoulders hunched. You look fucking pathetic. I thought you SAS guys were supposed to be something special. I thought you guys were supposed to be in good shape. Do you get back pain? Your posture is the worst I've ever seen.'

Then the woman chimed in: 'Are you cold, Trooper Fennell?'

Considering that I had recently been pulled from a freezer, I most definitely was cold, but I knew what she was getting at. She wasn't enquiring after my wellbeing; this session was obviously designed to humiliate the captive and shatter his self-esteem.

The man continued: 'You're a fucking disgrace. Stand up straight. Have a bit of pride in yourself.'

'And he's cold,' said the woman. 'Trooper Fennell, do you know why I *know* you're cold?'

I didn't reply.

'Trooper Fennell, answer me,' said the woman.

'I can't answer that question,' I replied.

'Look down. Go on, I want you to look at yourself,' said the woman, her face as cold and ugly as a rotting corpse. 'Do it!' she yelled.

I glanced down at my naked body, purely to keep the mongrel bitch at bay, but I didn't bother focusing on my penis or testicles. I had a good idea where my testicles were – probably somewhere in my stomach. This little session was doing wonders for my self-esteem. I decided to zone out and leave the interrogators for a while.

One soldier who had completed RTI training the previous year had reacted a little differently. This guy – unlike myself, of course – was a chronic masturbator. When the female interrogator made derogatory comments about his manhood, he began to touch himself. The woman left the room and he was given a mud bath.

I could still vaguely hear the interrogators yelling at me.

'You're a disgrace to the Australian army,' spat the man.

'You must be freezing, Trooper Fennell,' added Miss Sarcastic.

'Stand up straight. Take some pride in yourself, you sack of shit.'

'Don't be shy. Are you embarrassed?'

'Look at his posture. You've got the physique of a scrawny old man.'

'A scrawny, cold man,' said the woman.

Their comments continued – a flurry of lefts and rights that lacked any real punch. I visualised how hard I had pushed myself over the years. With my mind's eye I reread a Christmas card from my first martial arts instructor:

> *Keith,*
>
>   *I am so proud that you have achieved your goal.*
>   *A black belt is a clear indication that you can overcome any hurdle in your life. You have the spirit of the mind and body.*
>   *Chief Instructor,*
>   *Chopper Charlie*

I remembered the countless hours my mates and I had spent on our knuckles doing push-ups, and how giving in to the pain and dropping to our knees was not an option, because to give up would have been to let Charlie down. I remembered the disappointment on Charlie's face when I told him that I was leaving to pursue another martial art.

He didn't try to talk me out of it; he just thanked me and said he hoped I found what I was looking for.

I recalled being belted from one side of the hall to the other by Instructor Paul as he passed on some of the finer points of wing chun kung-fu. He regularly took me for one-on-one training at the end of class, which was a privilege that must be earned. Then there was the time when Paul palmed one of my students – also one of my mates – a little too firmly in the chest, fracturing his sternum in three places.

I might have looked naked and vulnerable on the outside, but mentally I recalled Charlie's words: 'Power of the mind and body . . . power of the mind and body . . .'

I felt untouchable after that.

≡

Later that evening I was moved into a hot room and made to do a physical training session with the other captives – my mates. Although I was blindfolded, I could hear the

A street march and demonstration shortly after achieving my first black belt.

others being abused, bastardisation at its best. At first we were made to do a combination of sit-ups and push-ups. After I had completed several sit-ups someone grabbed my knees and ripped my legs apart. We were already naked but this person obviously wanted to see more. This continued every three or four sit-ups. And while I was doing push-ups, what I expect were the same hands grabbed my hips and rammed my genitals into the ground in a fucking motion.

This degrading experience continued over and over again. It began to feel somewhat personal. I was certain that some sick prick was getting off on this, so when those dirty hands grabbed my knees for the umpteenth time I quickly raised my goggles, eyeballed the degenerate and whispered: 'I know who you fucking are,' before replacing my goggles and continuing with the exercises.

The weasel didn't say a word but his eyes were frozen with fear. I knew I had his measure. The degenerate left me alone, but others weren't so lucky.

The interrogators honed in on one individual and began a tirade of abuse. I knew the guy they were targeting. Their rants were raw, humiliating and personal. The man snapped, removed his goggles and threatened his captors. Our session concluded soon after that.

After another sleepless night and 32 to 36 hours in captivity, I was led outside and forced to kneel down. As the gravel pierced my knees, the sun kissed my back – a paradoxical moment of torment and pleasure. My hands were cuffed behind my back, and my head was lowered close to the ground. A guard removed my earmuffs and goggles, revealing a single piece of white bread on the ground before me.

'Eat,' he said.

I hadn't eaten anything since well before my capture, so I forced my face onto the stale piece of bread. Fearing it might be taken from me, I sucked the entire slice into my mouth and tried to chew. The little saliva I had was soon absorbed into the bread, which became a large dry ball. Swallowing was now impossible and I began to choke on the dry bread, dry-retching, with my hands still cuffed behind me.

'He's choking,' said one of the guards.

'Greedy fuck,' said another, removing my cuffs to allow me to dig the bread from my mouth. Hunched over half a dozen soggy bread balls, I devoured the slice like a dog, albeit in more manageable portions.

Later that morning I was questioned by two male interrogators. For 40 hours I had given them the big four and nothing more. Halfway through the session, one of the interrogators – the guy with the porno moustache – threw a tennis ball to me, which I instinctively caught with my right hand.

The two went into instant celebration, congratulating each other for making me crack. They appeared so excited that for a moment I thought they might try to fuck each other. When the euphoria settled down the man with the porno moustache said: 'You're right-handed. You've tried so hard to give nothing away, and now, just like that, we know you're right-handed.'

Not thinking straight, I responded: 'Yeah, well you could have worked that out by looking at my weapon.'

Damn it, I thought immediately after, realising that I'd taken their bait. But rather than allowing myself to become frustrated for making a mistake, I decided to move on and forget about it. I made certain that I answered the next question I was asked correctly. And the one after that, and the one after that. The guards were relentless.

'You fucked up and said yes. We've got it on camera!'

'We've got ya', you fucking screw-up!'

'You told us you were right-handed and you said yes! Now, what's your rank?'

'Private,' I replied.

'Come on, you've already fucked up. Just be honest. What's your rank?'

'Private.'

One of the interrogators pushed me down onto a chair. The other – the man with the porno moustache – continued: 'You're scared, aren't you? I can see your heart beating in your chest. Look down and take a look for yourself.'

I kept staring at the man's forehead, slightly cross-eyed so as to blur his face.

'Fucking look down, you fucking chicken shit!' exploded the man. He became enraged, yelling into my face from less than a foot away. He grabbed my arm and wrote *BROKEN* on it with a thick black marker pen. 'If this was real then I would have broken your arm, you lying fuck. What's your rank?'

'Private.'

'You fucking liar!' The man closed in again. 'What's your fucking rank, you –'

While he was in mid-sentence, I locked eyes with the man, angled my forehead towards his nose and slightly cocked my shoulder, as if I was about to smash him in the face.

His voice broke. 'You . . . you chicken shit.' His eyes flickered and broke contact with mine, and his Adam's apple rose and fell as he swallowed a mouthful of nervous tension. He knew I'd heard his voice waver. He knew he'd been unable to maintain eye contact, and he knew I'd seen him swallow.

I rocked back on my chair, knowing that I had, without really trying, just scared the shit out of the man with the porno moustache.

'Guards!' he yelled. 'Get him out of here.'

=

In my experience, it's the eyes – the type of stare and the size of the eyes – that reveal the most about a person. Large, vacant eyes might indicate that a person is overwhelmed or terrified. Their decision-making may be slow, poor or even non-existent. I have seen this numerous times in many different situations, from soldiers parachuting or coming under enemy fire for the first time, to soldiers conducting close-quarter battle training, where they are expected to make decisions rapidly in stressful situations. I have also seen it with children in the surf, or with elite sportspeople who are taken out of their comfort zones.

For me, however, the eyes that remain the most vivid – the eyes that I can visualise with perfect clarity, although it has been almost a decade since we locked stares – belong to the first man I killed in combat. He is now gone, but that intense stare of complete and utter panic will remain burned into my memory until my own eyes become dust.

Yes, the eyes can reveal many things about a person. Eyes of hatred cut like blades. Eyes of determination are sharp and focused. Eyes of sadness are narrow and moist, while eyes of love are soft and bright. The interrogator's eyes during that final RTI session were sheepish, jittery and distant.

Upon reflection, our interrogators were highly intelligent men. A couple of these guys should be nominated for an Oscar, such was their ability to hold character. But I'm certain there was at least one individual who got off on what they were doing. The person who continuously ripped my legs apart, grabbed my hips and rammed my genitals into the ground seemed a little too enthusiastic. He was either a brilliant actor who should be in Hollywood, or a filthy prick who was taking mental pictures for self-gratification.

≡

If I was to rate all my experiences, then the most uncomfortable to endure was, without doubt, extreme thirst. After that sits cold, then hunger. Next comes a lack of sleep or, in this case, sleep deprivation. Following the interrogation session with the man with the porno moustache, I was forced to sit with my legs crossed, my hands on my knees and my head straight for the next six to eight hours.

Including our time on patrol prior to being captured, we had not slept in 60 hours. Twenty-four hours without sleep is no more difficult than a big night out. After two days and two nights without sleep, things begin to get a little blurred. On the third day, after several adrenaline-inspired highs and lows, rigorous physical sessions and three or four interrogation sessions, you become somewhat delirious. We couldn't pop a pill or down a strong coffee. Sitting there unstimulated, fighting to remain awake for hours on end, is probably as punishing as counting from 1 to 1,000,000 and back again.

Dreaming about sex wasn't an option either. Sitting there naked and rocking to and fro with an erection would probably bring a bit more time in the freezer – no thanks.

I began to dream of sleep in the same way I occasionally used to dream of urination as a child. I remember fighting that lower ache and arguing with my subconscious mind. *Is the toilet before me bona fide, or is it just a façade? I'm not dreaming. I'm at school, standing in front of a toilet, dickie in hand, ready to let go. I've checked, double-checked.* I squeeze my penis. *This is real.*

The instant relief of letting go is soon replaced by panic as I wake up, mortified, pissing all over myself. Lying in soppy sheets and pyjamas as the sickly waft of piss penetrates the night air was like a shot of caffeine. I was no longer confused – I was without question very much awake!

=

I fought to remain conscious, my neck snapping back and forth, as sleep, like a drug, began to take control. As I began to hallucinate from lack of sleep, my mind drifted back to other times in my life. I remembered my other grandfather, Gerard, and how he used to challenge me when we went running, although he was almost 70 years old.

I recalled the look on my father's face when he told my ma that he found John, one of his closest mates, slumped over a machine and dead, electrocuted. I remembered walking along the railway tracks with my next-door neighbour and his dog. The high-pitched scream of a train's horn still evokes an image of my friend, hunched-over, palefaced, his mouth open and screaming. The metallic chattering sounds of the train overpowered his voice. His dog panicked and was cut in half.

When you're in the bag, you have a lot of time to think. The memories that kept me company were not always pleasant or logical. They were generally the more emotional or dramatic experiences of my life. Now, at the age of 35, I have a far greater reservoir of experiences, but then, as a 22-year-old, I used my past to garner strength.

Our guards must have found this phase of the training rather amusing. First the head would tilt, and then the neck would relax, allowing the head to fall. I would wake up, disoriented, unsure of where I was. The pressure around my eyes and over my ears from the goggles and muffs became accentuated over the hours. My head felt like it was clamped into a vice, and my knees like they were squashed beneath a bus.

And then came sleep. The relief, the euphoria of falling asleep, allowed my body to relax. With my chin nestled against my chest, I pumped deep, slow breaths into the air. I was asleep. I was free. Life had never been so good.

Slap!

Huh, what was that? Where the fuck am I? I thought. My breathing intensified. My heart revved hard as I tried to remember where I was. I attempted to touch my stinging forehead, but my hands did not respond. *Where are my hands?* I could not feel them – they were numb. I pushed my head onto my shoulder in an attempt to remove the pressure from my cheekbones, and a needle of light pierced my blacked-out world.

This is RTI training. I must have fallen asleep. My head aches because I'm wearing goggles and earmuffs. My knees aren't smashed or broken. They're sore because they're twisted and crossed, like they were back at school. I heard fading footsteps. *One of the guards must have slapped me. Fuckers.*

My body relaxed and my heart slowed as the shot of adrenaline dissolved into my system. Once again I duelled with sleep. And once again my mind succumbed as I drifted from reality.

The guards probably waited a couple of minutes before stalking their prey again. With silent steps they approach the dozing man, taking extreme care so as not to wake him. Once alongside their victim, they might signal to the other guards that they're ready to attack. They might even rehearse the strike, teasing themselves – a bit of foreplay. Then, when they can't restrain themselves any longer, they slap the sleeping man in the forehead and watch as their victim snaps from the surreal to the real.

Over the course of the afternoon, the guards, who were probably just bored, kept themselves amused by increasing the intensity of the forehead slaps. I decided to look for some amusement too.

After sitting still for a while, I slowly lowered my head to my chest and took deep breaths, imitating sleep. Over my own muffled breaths, my ears hunted for sound. In my mind I pictured a guard creeping towards me. I was rather surprised when I heard a faint noise in front of me – a muffled laugh. My heart was beating hard as I thrust out both of my legs, my right heel connecting with something hard – possibly a shin. The guard made a startled noise and stumbled. I recrossed my legs and the footsteps drifted away.

My head continued to sway, tilt and fall as I plunged in and out of microsleeps. Hallucinations became as vivid as real life. A dull pain scrambled my mind.

A hand touched my shoulder, and another raised my earmuffs.

'Sleep,' said a voice, 'sleep.'

I'm dreaming, I thought. *I'll probably piss myself next.*

I was gently lowered to the floor. I had no idea if what I was experiencing was genuine. But the pain in my knees and lower back began to fade. *Perhaps this is real . . . they're letting us sleep,* I thought. I relaxed my mind and left the conscious world. I imagine the transition from one state to the next would have been no more than 10 seconds, probably less. Although my bed was a wooden floor, to this day I have never slept so deeply.

Fifteen minutes later my body was shaken violently and yanked to a seated position. *What the fuck is going on?* I thought, as I relaxed and fell back to the floor. Once again a pair of strong hands ripped me off the floor and slapped my hands against my knees. I was convinced that I'd been allowed to sleep because I had a broken arm, so I signalled towards my right arm before attempting to lie back down.

My earmuffs were lifted. 'Fucking sit up, arsehole, or you'll get a cold bath.'

Those words – 'arsehole' and 'cold bath' – helped with the orientation. I was now fully awake, as if snatched from the clouds and dropped onto a bed of broken glass. I felt nauseated from a combination of hunger, lack of sleep and a violent awakening. I would experience this abrupt wakening many more times over the years to come, from rockets zinging overhead in the middle of an Afghani night, to deafening explosions as bombs and rockets pounded Baghdad's International Zone. My instinctive reaction was always to grab my weapon; in Afghanistan it was a Para Minimi, and in Baghdad a Glock 17 pistol that I kept on a drawer next to my bed. But during RTI training we just had to sit there and play the game.

A guard pulled me up off the floor and I responded by falling back over. I had little sensation in my legs; the hours sitting cross-legged had restricted the circulation to my lower limbs. The guard, convinced I was messing with him, pulled me to my feet and tried to drag me across the room. Again my legs collapsed beneath me.

'Stand up!' yelled the guard as he pulled my arms high behind my back. I groaned as my shoulder joints found new levels of flexibility.

'Stand up!'

I leant back and made the guard support my weight. He struggled to keep me off the ground, his awkward hands fumbling over my body. The guard seemed uncomfortable, not knowing how to support a naked man. I remember finding this amusing. Another guard came to assist, grabbing a handful of hair and my elbow.

This was a welcome distraction from the deep burn that radiated throughout my lower limbs as a rush of blood gave them life. I hobbled – was dragged – across the wooden floor and down several steps to the familiar gravelled surface. The pebbles were sharp and the night was cold.

We walked for 164 paces. I remember because, for whatever reason, I decided to count them. *100 plus the age of my grandfather when he died*, I thought. I was pushed to the ground. Lying there, my genitals squashed against the gravel, I heard the distinctive *whop whop whop* of a Huey helicopter. My handcuffs were removed as the *whops* became louder. I held my breath as the Huey landed close by, the rotor wash peppering my body with small stones and grit. I wondered where the guards were and hoped that they were copping it too. I guess they were nearby, as I was soon yanked to my feet and buckled into the Huey. The rotors increased in velocity and the Huey lifted into the air.

How fucking cold is it? I thought. The wind seemed to cut my skin like shards of ice. I sat hunched over, my head down and my arms pulled tight against my chest. I raised my goggles and noticed that I was on the starboard side of the helicopter. I looked to my right and saw a large man in a helmet seated beside me. He glanced in my direction, noticed I had raised my goggles and turned his head away. *He's not one of them*, I thought. *He's just the loadmaster.*

I turned my head to the left and saw three familiar shadowy figures squashed side by side. I reached over and tugged the hair of one. The startled man, still wearing goggles, raised his head and flicked it nervously from side to side. I laughed and did it again. I grabbed another one of the boys on the shoulder and gave a friendly squeeze. This man raised his goggles and spun around. It was dark but he was grinning, his white teeth reflecting the minimal light. He raised an earmuff and whispered something to the man whose hair I had pulled.

The loadmaster then decided enough was enough

and signalled for us to replace our goggles. I obliged and returned to darkness. With my vision gone, there was little to focus on other than the cold.

≡

The next 24 hours of RTI training were to be less physically exacting than the first two days, but I found it an even greater test of my self-belief. During our first 48 hours in captivity, we were subjected to three or four alternate interrogation techniques. Some guys who divulged information were interrogated up to a dozen times. During my more vulnerable moments, I thought about my heritage, what type of person I was, things I had achieved and who I wanted to be. At times I did begin to doubt some decisions, especially my declaration of my rank as private rather than trooper, but I did not let this affect my self-esteem; despite the physical and emotional abuse, I still backed my decision.

In life, there are always going to be detractors – armchair critics, usually – who say something can't be done or who criticise those who push the boundaries. But as I see it, if you don't believe in yourself, how can you expect anyone else to?

Following our joyride, I was escorted across a gravel surface and told to stand still. The night air seemed to lack commitment in contrast to the wind chill we'd experienced in the back of the Huey. I was still naked and cold, but the shuffling sounds around me suggested that something was different.

Then a man spoke. 'Remove your goggles.'

I followed his instructions and saw that I'd been lined up

with eight other soldiers from my troop. It also appeared that we were now in a mock prisoner-of-war (POW) camp. I briefly locked eyes with a couple of guys and observed that they looked just as dishevelled as I felt. I was shocked at their condition. We had only been in captivity for 48 hours, yet the men appeared to have aged considerably. Besides their haggard hair, the lack of sleep had left their faces lined and their eyes sunken and red. Our group ranged from 22 to 30 years of age. Fortunately I wasn't the youngest, so I was not required to take part in the first ridiculous exercise. Our troop commander was given a thick, black jacket – which looked very warm – and Evo, the youngest member of our troop, was told to pick off the fluff.

Evo is an intelligent man with great common sense. He is currently employed in Kabul but he lives in Brazil with

Evo running Colleen through the Heckler & Koch MP5 on an SAS family day in Perth.

his partner and young daughter. Growing up with three brothers and being educated in a boys' boarding school provided Evo with the edge he needed for military life. But as he readily admits, any outward display of affection does not come naturally.

Evo is a perfectionist. He's driven, works hard and is able to think clearly under pressure. Like Todd, he was well suited to close-quarter battle training, as his ability to think on his feet enabled him to make a decision quickly. The three of us would later be selected in the lead water-assault team on counter-terrorism duties. Evo was also calm underwater, a pleasure to work with when we had to dive in heavy seas, poor visibility or shark-infested waters.

During the first phase of RTI, Evo had assessed the time very accurately. Whenever he was outside, he would gauge the intensity of the sun; after 48 hours in captivity he was within a couple of hours of the correct time. Most guys had no idea.

Watching Evo pick the fluff off the Boss' coat was mildly entertaining. It was a peculiar task designed to establish an order of seniority. A few guys sniggered, but I remember feeling very much on-guard, so I adopted a vague persona and remained alert. During the next 24 hours our interrogators would attempt to divide our group, to fracture our team and create alienation. They would achieve their aim.

8

POW CAMP: OSTRACISING THOSE WHO RESIST

Feeling like an outsider, like you don't belong, is something most people experience in life. Children who are always last to be picked on a sporting team, immigrants from very different cultures, and those in same-sex relationships are some of the more extreme cases of those who experience alienation. A child who is bullied or ostracised over a lengthy time can become withdrawn, lose his or her confidence and suffer from low self-esteem. If someone is told something enough times, then they'll probably begin to believe it.

For 48 hours our interrogators verbally abused and degraded us. Most SAS soldiers are confident men with strong personalities, so the individual abuse we suffered had only a limited effect. But now, in the mock prisoner-of-war (POW) camp, where we were in a team environment, the interrogators attempted to divide our loyalty to the group by ostracising certain men.

My memory of the precise details of the camp commandant's opening address remains vague. The commandant was a 'grey man', more mediocre than impressive, and so his appearance largely eludes me. He had a full head of dark hair, perhaps greying a little on the sides, and a lean build. But I do remember his eyes – not their colour but the intensity of his stare. It was difficult to ascertain what the man was thinking. I had only noticed this a few times before.

The commandant introduced himself, informed us that we were prisoners of war and warned us that we must abide by the camp rules if we wished to be treated in accordance with the Geneva Convention. He also stressed that our interrogation sessions had concluded. He was very clear about this: 'Your interrogation is complete. You must now work together as a team. If you do not work together or if someone breaks the rules, then the group will be punished.'

Soldiers are selected for the SAS largely on their ability to work together during adverse conditions. When we heard that the commandant wanted us to work as a team, we naively believed that these next 24 hours would be relatively straight-forward.

But sneakily – or masterfully – the camp commandant had no intention of allowing us to work together. From the outset the interrogators' aim was to continue to gather information; and if any man resisted, he would be ostracised and made to feel like he wasn't contributing to the team – that he was letting his mates down. What better way was there to disrupt a committed team of men than to attack the very ideals on which they most prided themselves?

≡

We were soon ordered to line up and sign for a pair of pyjamas. I had no intention of signing anything, and I discussed this with Evo and Pete. The senior member of our group – an officer – was then chastised by the commandant for failing to control his men.

This was clever. If the guards could seed self-doubt in the mind of the boss about his own ability to lead, then he might lose sight of what the interrogators were trying to achieve. It was a successful ploy. The Boss ordered the rest of us to sign for our pyjamas. In the military you have to sign when issued equipment. This was, apparently, just routine.

I stood at the back of the line and when it was my turn, I picked up the pen in my non-dominant hand – my left – and scratched an X on the page. I then looked into the eyes of the man who was playing the enemy quartermaster and waited for his reaction. I saw him glance at my 'signature' before handing over a pair of oversized pyjamas. *Why didn't he say anything?*

Upon reflection, it should have been obvious to me why he ignored my protest. Our captors had already received a number of signatures, so to press for one more might alarm our group; they didn't want us to realise that they were still gathering information. Our captors wanted each man to relax, to drop his guard. After that, the information – polluted and toxic – should flow like the Ganges.

The intelligence officers were highly skilled, experts at manipulation. They had a plan, were well-drilled and were working together to achieve their aim. In contrast, we were prisoners who had not slept in three days and had to react to the commands of others. We were also not permitted to speak to one another. Whenever the guards saw someone speak, the entire group – except that individual – was

punished. With no ability to communicate, we were unable
to formulate a plan. And with no plan, we were isolated.

During the next 24 hours numerous scenarios were
played out. At one point we met with a mock representa-
tive of the Red Cross. We were seated in a large room
behind individual desks arranged in neat lines – it was
like a schoolroom. The Red Cross rep flashed us some
identification before beginning his performance. He was
charismatic, funny and sincere. This man was so sympa-
thetic to what we'd gone through that anyone would have
thought he'd been there with us.

He said he would try to improve our living conditions
and would see if he could get us something to eat. When
he asked what we'd like, he was bombarded with wishful
requests. I sat there and said nothing. It was pointless
contributing to the conversation – there was no way this
man was going to be able to source KFC or pizza, as the
men were requesting.

The Red Cross rep asked general questions to the group,
to see who would respond. He then targeted individuals, first
those who were willing to talk and then those who were
not. I scanned the room behind him, searching for cameras
or anything unusual. He asked me how I was; I just raised my
shoulders, as if to suggest I didn't know. He was clever. Sens-
ing my resistance, he immediately targeted someone else. His
aim was to establish rapport and trust. Pressing the wrong
person for too long could have meant that the others might
cotton on and also withdraw from the conversation.

When he left the room I tried to communicate my
concern to my mates: I believed they were still gathering
information. A man then burst into the room and

demanded to know who had spoken. I said nothing, and so we were punished as a group.

We all looked ridiculous in our pyjamas. The waistband of my pants was more than double the size required. The elastic had been removed, so I was forced to tie the pants in a knot to stop them from falling down. The result: a baggy crotch and permanent wedgie.

While foreign music blared from some loudspeakers, we were ordered to construct a vegetable garden. I didn't have a problem with this. Scratching at the surface of the dry earth with inadequate gardening tools kept me warm. Some guys began to laugh, both at the hideous music and at the way their mates looked with their pyjamas tied around their stomachs like a group of belly-dancers. We were only permitted to speak to the prisoner whom our captors had placed in charge. He was to be addressed by his surname prefixed by the word 'brother'. Brother Fennell was never placed in charge.

Our captors allowed some joviality. When smartarse questions like: 'This music is good for our morale – is it possible to increase the volume?' were asked, our captors responded with witty comebacks that were sometimes hilarious. The more relaxed we were, the easier it would be for them to extract information.

We were then seated together on the floor in a small room, where we were addressed and engaged in conversation by another man. Although he looked different, I recognised him from one of my previous interrogation sessions. He was the man whose voice had broken when I eyeballed him. He asked us questions about the Sally Man – an iconic and much-loved figure in the Australian military who would turn up out bush and provide soldiers with biscuits and brews. Everyone loves the Sally Man. It was then that I was targeted a little more aggressively.

'So, Fennell, tell me about the Sally Man.'

I just grinned a dumbarse grin and looked at the floor.

'Fennell, what's wrong – don't you like the Sally Man?'

The man's accent was even more ridiculous than the ones I'd heard on selection. I just nodded my head.

'You do or you don't?'

Once again I just raised my shoulders.

'What we have here is someone who won't contribute to the team. Why won't you contribute, Fennell?'

I stared at the floor.

'Oh, we have a sulker?' said the man. 'Someone's not happy. Perhaps you find it stressful here? The others don't appear stressed.'

This was brilliant work by our captor. There were sniggers throughout the room. I was now being ostracised, beginning to be made to feel inferior to the rest of the group.

The man left the room and I finally spoke: 'Don't you guys see that these fuckers are still gathering information?'

'You feeling a little bit stressed, Keithy?' was one jeering reply. A couple of other guys laughed.

I could see what was happening and I found it deeply frustrating. For failing to contribute – that is, to provide information – I was being vilified as a non-team player, someone who was too uptight. With every mocking comment from our captors – many of which were genuinely droll – a couple of my peers had chimed in and taken the piss.

A man then entered the room and yelled at me for speaking. My mates were ordered outside and made to do push-ups on the dirt while I watched.

'You men are being punished because one of your own does not respect the camp rules. He spoke, knowing that if caught, you would all be punished. It is clear that this man is an individual who does not respect others.'

The leader of our group was then abused and stood down. I was placed in isolation.

Our captors unwittingly did me a favour, since the time alone allowed me to gather my thoughts without distraction. I reflected deeply. No one enjoys feeling like an outsider, and for an SAS soldier, being accused of being a non-team player is up there with being considered suspect under fire. As much as I wanted to join my mates and blend in with the group, I decided to follow my instincts and provide our captors with as little information as possible.

When I was released I rejoined the group back in the vegetable garden. The officer who had been deposed had a quiet word in my ear; he ordered me to 'play the game'.

'Can't you see what's going on, Boss?' I said, irritated that now I was being ordered to divulge information.

'The interrogation is over. We're in a POW camp and I'm ordering you to play the game.'

I turned to the other officer in the group and reiterated my thoughts. He seemed a little more receptive. I could see him thinking about it, nodding his head but continuing to stare at the ground.

Our captors, however, were diligent and were always on the lookout for anyone talking. They didn't want us to work together anymore. The group was punished again, and it was no surprise that I was made to watch.

We were then taken to the room with the desks and encouraged to sing. 'Music and song are good for morale,' we were told. It was like karaoke but without alcohol. I remained quiet and watched the show.

'Who's next?' said our captors. I rolled my eyes and waited for the obvious. 'What about you, Fennell? Would you like to contribute to the team?'

'Come on, Keithy,' said one of the boys.

I placed my head down on the table and waited for the mocking to begin. It never came, as one of the boys – perhaps wanting to be crowned karaoke king – sang a country song loudly and out of tune.

Next we were told that we were allowed to write a letter to our loved ones, to inform them that we were alive and well. *You can't be serious*, I thought. *This is ridiculous. Surely no one here would be stupid enough to write a letter and address it home*. I was wrong. Portions of these letters were later read out during our debriefing session. Now that was funny.

We were given a piece of white paper and several coloured pencils. I realised that to do nothing would have been to make a statement, thus further alienating myself from the group. So I took a pencil and sketched a large rectangle. I drew lines across the diagonals and then neatly coloured in each triangle with a different colour. The drawing had no significance or meaning.

We were handed an envelope and told to insert our letter, seal the envelope and address it. I wrote a fictitious street name and left it at that. Our captors collected the envelopes and told us that they would be posted. In fact, they took them to another room and analysed them for intelligence.

Evo had written: 'If a tree falls in the woods and no one sees or hears it fall, then does it really make a noise?' The interrogators thought he had lost his mind and were so concerned that they spoke with his patrol commander, who pissed himself laughing and said: 'I told him to write that as a message to me.'

$$\equiv$$

We were exhausted, almost delirious. We had only slept for about 15 minutes in nearly 84 hours. It is little wonder guys were singing and writing letters home.

In the afternoon we were allowed to sit on our beds but were not permitted to lie down or sleep. Our captors had made a few changes to our seniority, promoting troopers and demoting officers. Those in command were afforded additional privileges.

Pete, a mate of mine, approached me, slapped me on the shoulder and said: 'Well done, mate. You've been fucking staunch.'

Any self-doubt I had instantly disappeared. I had enormous respect for Pete. He was a hard man who could physically extend himself further than most. He gave 100 per cent in everything he did, whether it was soldiering, training or consuming alcohol. Even after a big night he was always in the lead group on a troop PT session.

Pete was passionate about soldiering – he was a natural warrior who always put others ahead of himself. Whenever a volunteer was needed for a shitty job, Pete would be the first to raise his hand. I know I disappointed him when I made the decision to leave the green machine. In fact, I could tell he was a little pissed off because we were good mates – I was one of his groomsmen – and I hadn't discussed it with him. Essentially, I hadn't wanted to be dissuaded by men who loved soldiering as much as I did.

If I had to pick a team of men to join me in war, it would be made up of men I know would remain by my side, whatever was going down. There is no doubt that Pete, for his loyalty alone, would be in that team.

Pete later told me that while he was being interrogated, he had started to believe the captors' abusive rhetoric. I had too, especially when they told me how pathetic I looked. They had told Pete that he might as well open up, as his mate Fennell had told them everything.

'You know, mate,' Pete told me, 'that's where they fucked up. I knew you wouldn't say shit. After that, nothing they said affected me.'

It would have been the same if they'd said something like that to me. Before we went into the bag, our patrol 2IC said to Pete and me: 'Just remember, guys, big four and nothing more, or you're a weak cunt.'

Pete and I shook hands and recited the words. I knew Pete would never break, not ever.

The Boss continued to get a hard time for failing to control his men. Once again he told me that our interrogation sessions were over, and once again he told me to play the game. I shook my head. We were both tired and had read the situation differently.

It was late afternoon, the final hour before the sun knocked off, when I was once again summoned outside.

I saw a man with a video camera filming one of the boys – our new leader – while he discussed the finer points of abseiling. The camera then turned on me.

'Now you will show us,' they demanded.

I was tired, and fed up with confrontation. It would have been far easier to just go along with their tiresome game, but I couldn't. I thought about what the Boss had said. I then thought about Pete's comments. He gave me strength.

Here we go, I thought. *Back in isolation.* I shook my head and spat: 'I don't have to and will not be filmed,' before attempting to walk off.

One of the guards stopped me, grabbing my face and aggressively forcing it towards the camera. Now I was beginning to get really pissed. I pushed the camera away and yelled again: 'I'm not doing it!'

I was ordered to return to the accommodation hut. We all were. Once inside, we were told to sleep. But I was furious – sleep would be impossible.

Twenty minutes later, one of our captors approached me and asked me to follow him outside.

'I told you, I'm not doing it,' I said.

'Follow me,' said the man.

Once we were outside, another intelligence officer introduced himself and told me the training was over. Naturally, I didn't believe him.

'Look, you were right,' he said. 'We were still gathering information. You guys haven't had any sleep for nearly four days, so congratulations, mate, you did well. Our aim was to create conflict and isolate those who continued to resist. It'll all come out in the debriefing session later. For now, I want you to calm down – don't try to escape. Just go back to your room and get your head down. You're gonna need it.'

I still couldn't trust him but I calmed down, returned to my bed and slept. *These guys are switched on*, I thought, as it had indeed crossed my mind to break out. Evo, Pete and I had even begun to discuss options.

Two hours later an SAS troop – our mates – raided the camp and we escaped. The next phase of our training – escape and invasion – would last for another 72 hours.

We were given our boots, a water bladder and one set of military fatigues. We found some hessian sacks, cut a hole for our head and secured them around our waists – an attempt to stave off the cold. We walked for most of that night, covering almost 20 kilometres, before trying to sleep under a large water pipe that runs between Northam and Perth. The cold earth sucked the heat from one side of our bodies while the ferocious wind stripped it from the other.

'Hey, Fenno, are you asleep?' asked my patrol 2IC.

'Hell no,' I replied.

'We couldn't hear you rolling around so thought you were either asleep or dead.'

I laughed.

'You cold?' he asked.

'Freezing . . . too cold to sleep,' I said.

'Pull it in with us, mate.'

The five of us huddled tight. I had never spooned with another male before, but right then I would have spooned with my old man if it had meant I was going to be a little warmer.

The next day we met an agent, who provided us with

shelter and food. We would lie up during the day and move at night. Over the next two days we followed the pipe towards Perth, covering a total distance of just over 50 kilometres.

≡

During our debrief, the intelligence officers informed us that each of the three troops in our squadron were vastly different. Mine was identified as the water troop, as we were slightly more aggressive and extroverted by nature. *This was true*, I thought as my mind returned to the morning we had to sing.

Next the intelligence officers discussed how they had attempted to create internal conflict within the group: 'When some soldiers continue to resist, it's likely that others will do the same. We attempt to ostracise these people and turn the group against them.' They mentioned my letter with the multicoloured rectangle and how they'd spent considerable time analysing it, before realising it was just an abstract, token contribution that gave nothing away. Initially they thought I had been subdued.

Finally, they told us how they had intentionally pressured those in leadership positions and attacked their ability to control the team; the aim was that the captured leaders would coerce their men to fall into line.

Strong leadership is vital, for without it a team will fragment into smaller and less effective groups. For example, Evo, Pete and I had all continued to resist, so we'd gravitated towards one another. We had even begun to discuss an escape.

This is why men who fail to display leadership potential are usually not accepted into the SAS. In my opinion, when working in small teams *everyone* must have the capacity to lead. A patrol 2IC must be able to assume control if his commander is killed or wounded. It is vital that the person filling this position is not just a sound administrator but a competent leader as well.

In the military, you're trained to follow orders, and if soldiers didn't respond to orders there would be anarchy. Just because a leader might make a decision you don't agree with doesn't give you the right to fly solo. Not everyone can lead, and not every decision a leader makes is going to be popular or even correct.

So when a poor command is issued, what is a soldier to do? I've learnt to choose my battles. If there is little at stake then I'll probably let it slide and save my energy for something more important. If it's important, your skills of persuasion come to the fore. Most people are open to advice, especially if it's for their own benefit and is delivered in a non-threatening, positive way.

The SAS isn't a 'Chinese parliament' – where everyone's opinion is worth an equal amount – but anyone in a patrol can and does contribute when a complex decision must be made. The strongest leaders I know are not driven by ego or intimidated by the abilities of others. They embrace the knowledge and ideas of those around them in order to establish the *best* course of action.

Often it's a commander who comes up with the right solution because of his superior experience, but sometimes it's the least experienced member of the team. He might bring something new, or have an ability to think outside the box. And of course there can be any number of hybrid solutions. When time permits, I believe this option offers the most diverse and rewarding results.

≡

During my time in the POW camp I made some mistakes. Rather than become frustrated when I was ordered to 'play the game', I should have been more discreet with my actions. The times when I made an obvious stand – my refusal to sing, to discuss the Sally Man or to allow myself to be filmed – ended with me being targeted and ostracised. Conversely, the times when I was more prudent in my refusal to engage – such as when I signed my name with an X, or when I drew the multicoloured box instead of writing a letter – enabled me to blend into the group without giving anything away.

Overall, it was a huge test of my self-belief. Having our captors, a superior and several colleagues challenge my actions, especially at a time when we were all deprived of sleep, did make me question my decisions. I took the time – when I was in isolation – to assess my thoughts. I had decided to back myself, and although I was concerned about being branded a non-team player, you should never follow a team if it's obvious they're headed in the wrong direction.

This is a message that I've tried to instil in my children: 'If you know something isn't right, then trust yourself and don't allow yourself to be pressured by anyone. To make a stand – to remain in control – requires far more courage than to jump aboard the popularity train to nowhere.'

9

HOSPITALS AND AFRICA: HUMANITARIAN OPERATIONS

While deployed to Indonesia on a special-operations training team in 1996, our troop – a conglomerate of soldiers from the water, freefall and mobility troops – took part in 'Binta', a task designed to win the hearts and minds of the local people, who had been providing us and the Kopassus – the Indonesian special forces – with fresh food.

An Indonesian commander organised a couple of favours for us to do in return. 'Tomorrow morning,' he said, 'everyone except the medics will be painting the mosque.'

I was a patrol medic so I grinned and tried not to laugh.

'Medics,' he continued, 'you are to meet at the clinic at 7 am with your medical packs. You'll be doing circumcisions.'

Did he just say circumcisions? I thought to myself. Most of the boys were still trying to come to terms with their job of painting a mosque, so no one really acknowledged the patrol medics' task. *Nah, he probably just made a mess of the translation.* I didn't give it another thought and continued to take the piss out of the painters.

The next morning, relieved to have dodged mosque-painting duties and under the guidance of a corps medic, three of us walked up the hill to the clinic, our med kits slung over our shoulders. We didn't know what we'd be doing and we didn't care. *Whatever it was, it had to be better than painting the mosque,* we thought. As we trudged along the heavily dewed track, I noticed a bunch of boys sitting outside the clinic – there were 17 in total. They were aged between about six and 14. The commander's previous words – 'doing circumcisions' – bounced between my ears like an echo.

'Did any of you guys hear the commander say we'd be doing circumcisions?' I asked.

'Yeah, but I thought he must have fucked up the translation.'

'Me too,' said another.

'They can't be serious,' I said.

For the village boys, the thought of being circumcised was terrifying: their pallid faces told us so. But for their parents and families, it was exciting, a time of celebration – an important initiation from boy to man.

A couple of Indonesian doctors were in charge of the operations and our job was to assist them. From the outset, their lack of hygiene and disregard for sterilisation posed a moral dilemma. The doctors weren't changing their gloves between operations, and their bloodied medical tools were used on one patient and then the next. We were horrified by the potential for cross-contamination. And apart from all that, in Australia many people – including medical practitioners – believed the operation itself was unnecessary and potentially harmful.

'Man, these guys are military doctors but they don't give a shite about hygiene,' I said. 'I'm all for gaining experience, but lopping off some poor kid's foreskin isn't what I had in mind.'

But we knew that, irrespective of what we thought or said, these boys were going to be circumcised. That was a given. We had a choice: we could refuse to take part and walk away, or we could employ our own stringent protocols of hygiene in an attempt to make the operations safer. We were all qualified to administer local anaesthetic and were competent in suturing – tying stitches. We unzipped our med packs, laid out our equipment and donned gloves.

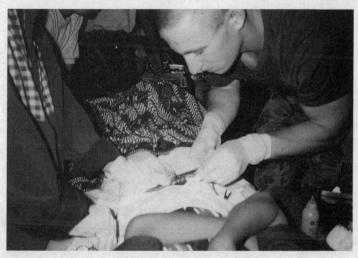

Moral dilemma: circumcisions in Indonesia.

While locking off the final suture on my first patient, I glanced at the boy's face to ensure he wasn't in any discomfort. I couldn't believe what I saw. The operation was not yet finished but a man who appeared to be the boy's grandfather had popped a cigarette into the corner of the child's mouth. I completed the stitch at the same time that a match sparked the cigarette to life. A coughing fit ensued.

'*Maaf pak, silakhan tunggu ya,*' I said – excuse me, sir, please wait.

The boy's grandfather just nodded his head in excitement.

I was more relieved than pleased with how the sutures looked. I'd taken my time. I wouldn't appreciate someone rushing stitches on my penis, and I'm sure this little guy would some day feel the same. I removed my gloves, shook the boy's hand and congratulated him for being very brave and strong. He smiled and I followed the doctor to the next bed.

≡

As qualified SAS patrol medics, we were required to spend a couple of weeks each year attached to a hospital casualty ward to enhance our skills. We were permitted to give inoculations, to take blood, to establish IV (intravenous) access, to suture and dress wounds, and to assist with anything else that needed doing. Taking blood or establishing IV access in elderly people or children is far more difficult than it is in SAS soldiers. Most of the boys in the troop have veins like drainpipes, but if a soldier suffers from shock or blood loss, their veins soon contract. Locating a vein in a trauma situation is more like establishing a line in a young child.

When treating a casualty, SAS soldiers are advised to go for the median cubital vein – the large vein in the crook of the arm – but if access is unfeasible due to severe trauma or hypovolemic shock, they are trained to perform a venous cutdown – an emergency procedure where an incision is made in the ankle to gain access to the veins. Rehearsing on an old unconscious sheep in the hour before it is put down is one thing, but actually cutting into a mate's leg would take a lot of self-belief, especially if it had been many years since your initial training had taken place. The anatomy of a sheep's throat is comparable to a human's, so we were trained on them to perform other life-saving procedures, such as a cricothyroidotomy – making an incision in the front of the throat and inserting a small tube to bypass a restricted airway.

While working in Royal Perth Hospital, I was paired up with a sixth-year medical student. We were both under the guidance of a senior nurse.

'Which one of you would like to establish an intravenous line in the young girl in bed three?' the nurse asked us.

I looked at the soon-to-be doctor, indicating I was keen but I was happy if he wanted to give it a crack. He shot me back a look that said: *No thanks – I'm shitting myself.*

'I'll give it a go,' I said.

I established the IV. 'Nice work, Keith,' said the nurse.

Then it was the young doc's turn. An elderly lady also required a line. The doc swabbed the site and removed a 20-gauge cannula from its packet. He was having trouble locating a vein.

'Remember to tighten the tourniquet,' said the nurse.

He turned to me and said: 'Is it okay if you wait outside, because I get really nervous with someone watching me?'

I thought he was joking and laughed.

He secured the tourniquet around the woman's upper arm, wiped the site with an alcohol swab and lined up the cannula. Just before he punctured the skin he stopped again and asked the nurse and me to leave. I rolled my eyes and walked away.

'That really hurts,' I heard the elderly woman say.

I knew he had blown it – when you punch through the vein there is an instant dull ache. I had experienced this countless times in training while one of my mates attempted to persuade an assessor that they were in the vein. Some would even go so far as to turn on the IV and squeeze the bag, forcing fluid underneath my skin. I'd try to smile and would say: 'Yeah, good job, you're in, mate.' But in reality, what I really wanted to say was: 'You dick! My arm's killing me and I'll be left with a haematoma the size of a golf ball!'

While conducting his medical requalification training in the Regiment, one mate pierced my arm with an 18-gauge cannula. Over the years my arms had been stabbed many dozens of times, but never had I experienced such a sharp and intense pain. I knew he had fucked it up, but even the nurse who was assessing him was initially confused by the brilliant flashback of blood that had shot into the cannula. As he argued with the nurse, telling her that he was in the vein, I had to turn away because the pain was contorting my face.

'I don't think you're in,' said the nurse. 'How does it feel, Keith? Do you feel any discomfort?'

Discomfort . . . If this idiot doesn't stop arguing then I might have to punch him in the face, I thought. 'Yep, feels pretty good to me,' I said as I grimaced from the pain.

'I'm in,' he said as he attached the line and turned on the IV. But rather than clear fluid flowing into my body, bright-red blood shot up the line and began to fill the bag. 'See, look at the flashback,' he said in a pissed-off tone.

'Remove the IV,' said the nurse. 'You've cannulated his artery.'

He looked at me and I nodded with a clenched jaw and large eyes.

'Jesus, sorry, man.' He removed the cannula but didn't apply any pressure to the puncture and a stream of blood pulsed through the air, painting the grass at least 10 metres away.

'Put pressure on it!' yelled the nurse.

'Man, when it's my turn to jab you I'm gonna stick the thing in your eye,' I said, laughing.

He tried again on my other arm. This time he was successful.

At the hospital another time, a young woman – a model – arrived. She'd been involved in a minor vehicle accident and required a couple of sutures in her forehead. A doctor asked if I would like to do it.

'No probs,' I said.

He asked me whether I had sutured before, and I told him that I had never stitched a person but had practised on slabs of pig skin. The doctor's eyes bulged and he politely said he would take care of this one. Later that evening, a drunken, abusive man came in with a busted nose. He also required stitches; this time, my pig-skin qualification was sufficient.

≡

After returning from my first operational deployment, in February 1998 – an anti-poaching task in the southern Indian Ocean – I was keen to gain more medical experience.

I decided to organise a trip of my own. At the time, SAS soldiers were encouraged to venture overseas in what were known as 'Amelio' deployments. The primary aim was for soldiers to gain additional knowledge and experience, thus enhancing the capability of the Regiment.

In the 12 months that the project had been active, only one other soldier had made a submission. Although I was still a relatively junior member of the unit, I was confident I would gain approval for either a medical deployment to Chole Island, a small island 20 kilometres east of Tanzania, or a trip to Johannesburg, where I'd be attached to a hospital casualty ward. The prospect of treating gunshot wounds in Johannesburg was enticing, but I chose Chole Island as I believed I would learn more under the supervision of a former SAS Regimental Medical Officer (RMO) who had established a small medical clinic on the island.

I have always been drawn to positive people who aren't afraid to put themselves out there. The Doc was one such person. To be selected as our RMO was a feat in itself, as the position is always one that attracts much competition. Not content with this, the Doc decided to complete the selection course so he could better understand what it was like for the soldiers who took part. He received no favouritism and I'm sure that like everyone else, he learnt a lot about himself along the way. He passed the course and hobbled back to work.

I typed up an Amelio proposal and submitted the paperwork to my squadron commander. It came back later that day covered in red ink. I worked through his suggestions and submitted version two. This version copped an even bigger hammering than the first. After three or four knockbacks I was starting to regret making the application. As it was, I was only asking for $815 to pay for my accommodation and the flights from Dar es Salaam to Mafia Island, and that I be exempt from our compulsory week of med training the following year. With the amount of red pen my proposal received, anyone would think I was asking for a fully funded Contiki tour around Europe.

My troop commander sensed my frustration. 'Hey, Fenno,' he said. 'If it makes you feel any better, I don't think I've ever handed the Boss a piece of paperwork that he hasn't hammered. He loves his red pen.'

I didn't realise it at the time, but my squadron commander was doing me a favour. Besides testing my perseverance, he was nurturing me through the process because he wanted me to attain maximum growth. I was thinking about medical work in Africa – small picture – he was thinking about the process of organising such a trip – big picture.

I resubmitted my proposal again and soon learnt that I would have to present my plan to half a dozen senior officers, including the commanding officer of the SAS. *You've got to be shitting me*, I thought. *Just writing it was bad enough, and now I've gotta sell the freaking thing to the main man?*

I knew there was no way I could pull my submission without looking like a pussy, so I went home and asked my wife if she could give me a hand with a PowerPoint presentation. At the time, my computer skills were pretty much non-existent. I acknowledged the shortfall and within four months was touch-typing at 60 words per minute.

The presentation Colleen put together was probably a decade ahead of its time. It was so slick it bordered on ridiculous. When it was over, the commanding officer made a point of saying it was one of the best presentations he'd ever seen. My smug smile vanished when my troop commander enlightened the group that it had been my wife who had put the masterpiece together.

But the commanding officer approved my proposal. I was off to Africa.

The Doc and his wife had invited Colleen to join me, and she didn't have to be asked twice. We flew to Dar es Salaam and searched for a taxi. After 20 minutes we took our chances and threw our packs in an old banged-up station wagon. It was white and had a piece of mauve carpet glued to the dash. With not a lot of cash to throw around, we'd chosen to stay at the Safari Inn. For US$15 we weren't expecting anything flash.

Our taxi driver appeared genuine, and his face was full and smooth. But when he veered off the main road and began taking way down a couple of poorly lit alleys, I looked at Col and shook my head. 'If this dude tries to pump us over then I promise I'll snap his bloody neck.'

I felt a little foolish. Although I knew there wouldn't be a lot I could do if a group of his mates were waiting around the corner, I felt better knowing that he'd also have a pretty shitty night. We continued on. The sides of the alley were lined with corrugated iron, and the street narrowed to the point where it was impossible to open both left and right doors at the same time. Our vehicle headlights illuminated the dusty, potholed road.

The driver stopped the car and pointed to a building with barred windows. 'Safari hotel over there. I go check.'

I was tempted to follow him. There were many dull glows hidden behind drawn curtains. An armed guard approached the driver, they had a conversation and the driver returned. He looked relieved and told us everything was arranged. It was only the second time I had seen him smile; the first had been when he offered us a ride. I paid him and asked if he would pick us up the following morning. For this we scored smile number three.

Our room was surprisingly spacious, with two single beds set on opposite sides.

'This is cool,' said Colleen as she jumped onto her bed and unravelled the mosquito net.

I checked my bed and felt like Poppa Bear – someone with sandy feet had been sleeping in my bed. 'Do you want to go out for a look around?'

'No way,' said Col.

'Come on, we're in Africa.'

With an armed guard downstairs, Col was happy to stay in the room while I went for a walk. I removed everything from my wallet except for $10. Not far from the hotel I met a couple of locals who offered me some weed. I declined, so they asked if I would like a beer instead. I nodded and opened up my wallet nice and wide. They checked the contents and one of them signalled for me to give him two dollars.

With this in hand, he ran off down the road while his mate patted the kerb, encouraging me to take a seat. He smiled and sucked hard on his joint. I wasn't expecting to see the man who ran off with my two dollars again, and I didn't expect that Mr Weed was going to hang around either.

A couple of minutes later, the man returned with three bottles of beer, from which the caps had already been removed. I offered them both a bottle but they shook their heads and pointed to their joint. I was sceptical about drinking from a bottle that had been opened so I was adamant they joined me. They agreed to take one bottle between them; the other two were for me.

Before I had finished my second beer, Mr Weed signalled for my wallet, opened it, took out another two dollars and handed the money to his mate, who once again ran off down the road. He returned my wallet to me and smiled.

An Italian man wearing a white shirt and safari pants soon joined us, and so did three Masai men, their skin as dark and rich as chocolate. They were dressed in traditional red robes, wore sandals and carried spears. They were cool guys, and the Italian was able to smooth the boundaries between English and Swahili. Over the next two hours Mr Weed opened and closed my wallet three more times. The Africans preferred to smoke pot, while the Italian and I drank beer.

Colleen, wondering where I had got to, tiptoed out of her room and followed the laughs that bounced through the corridors. She was confused: she recognised my laughter but had no idea where it was coming from. She pressed her ear against several doors before returning to her room and going to bed. Not long afterwards, I opened the door, all smiles. Not even the grit between my sheets annoyed me that night.

The next morning, dressed in black pants and a white collared shirt, the driver waited eagerly by his cab. He looked like he was dressed for church. I wasn't surprised; he'd charged us $50 the day before. To him, we were easy money.

We spent the morning at the airport, arguing with a local travel agency. First they tried to tell us that our flights to Mafia Island had not been paid for, then they said there were no flights that day, and finally, after nearly six hours of waiting and heated negotiation, we were escorted to a dodgy plane, an old six-seater Cessna, out the back.

The plane had been double-booked, and it was obvious that our fares were supplementing a few of the locals'. Little wonder they didn't want us on the plane – there wasn't room. But I was adamant we were getting on, so we squashed our packs in the outside luggage compartment and boarded.

Col was petrified and refused to sit up the front near the pilot. She preferred to sit behind me, where she could close her eyes and pretend she was somewhere else. With just three seats remaining, seven other people piled on board; one guy was carrying a cage with a couple of chickens. The turbulent flight from Dar es Salaam to Mafia Island took 45 minutes, and I don't know who hated it more – Col or the chickens.

We retrieved our packs and were met by the Doc's wife, Jackie. She was a tall, attractive woman with a tremendous work ethic and keen sense of adventure. The Doc's boyish smile juxtaposed his powerful physique, which was well suited to playing rugby. They both were strongly motivated people, not by money but to provide the residents of Chole with sustainable primary health care. We rattled across

Chole Island, East Africa.

Mafia Island in an old four-wheel drive, which only took about 40 minutes. Then we bundled our packs and supplies onto a wooden sailing boat and enjoyed the 20-minute ride to Chole Island itself.

Chole forms part of the Mafia Island group, located south of Zanzibar. Largely surrounded by mangroves interspersed with quaint stretches of beach, the island has a tropical climate that is perfect for an assortment of palm and baobab trees. Thick rainforest dominates the centre. There are two rainy seasons: the short rains from November to December, and the long rains from March to May. Eighty per cent of the island's 2000 mm of rainfall each year comes during the latter season.

No vehicles are permitted on the island, and with no power Chole remains a reminder of what life was once like for millions of Africans. When the light fades, a hush envelopes the island as the locals retreat into their mud-brick huts, with sleep not too far away.

Besides the medical clinic, which the Doc and Jackie established in late 1997, an eco-tourism lodge was also being constructed. The owners have since done a wonderful job establishing a series of stunning tree-houses that add to, rather than detract from, the island's natural beauty.

The 800 predominantly Muslim locals who lived on Chole Island appeared happy, their lives uncluttered and their days filled with fishing and subsistence farming. The Doc's residence had a biblical feel; a gravel path bordered by white coral led to a brilliant white building. Two red bougainvilleas dominated the entrance. The place looked so clean and so pure that for a moment I thought I might be refused entry unless I wiped the dust from my boots. But the goat shit that littered the front steps made me feel more at ease.

We arrived on 10 January 1999. The following morning I accompanied the Doc to the medical clinic, a 600-metre trek through the rainforest. By the time we reached the clinic my trousers and shirt were damp, my forehead shiny with perspiration. The clinic, small and clean, comprised two examination rooms, a birthing suite, laboratory, undercover waiting area, toilet and several storerooms. The floors, even in the waiting area, were concrete. The examination rooms had a couple of chairs, a wooden desk and a long examination table, which had been sanded smooth and painted with lacquer.

The staff were well trained and friendly. Although they only had a fairly limited grasp of English, what they did know was sufficient when translating between us and the locals.

Training for the local staff, Chole Island.

My first patient, a man aged in his mid-thirties, complained of numbness in his legs. The Doc waited until I'd asked a series of questions before telling me he was suffering from a disorder, Guillaine-Barré syndrome, which affected his bowels and limbs.

'Fenno, as you'll see, we're only able to provide limited treatment on the island. This man might never regain full sensation in his lower limbs. The main problem is infection, as he'll most likely cut his foot at some point and won't feel it.'

We gave the man a course of multivitamins and told him to regularly check the soles of his feet. There was nothing else we could do.

My next patient was a fisherman who had stepped on a nail. I cleaned and dressed the wound and sent him on his way. The next man, wearing a sarong and a loosely buttoned white shirt, hobbled into the examination room, propped himself up on the table and spread his legs. *A regular*, I thought.

The man smiled and revealed a dressing on the inside of his upper right thigh. What had begun as a minor graze had now degenerated into a deep tropical ulcer. I removed the dressing and held my breath as I inspected the wound. The stench, like a rotting mouse, was vile. A thin piece of sterile cloth – a wick – protruded from the wound.

'With something like this, it's better to allow the wound to drain,' the Doc said. 'We inserted a wick four days ago and he's come back to have it replaced. Even minor cuts can turn into deep ulcers in the tropics. Unless it's a clean cut, the best way to treat them is with either secondary healing or delayed primary closure.'

I took the end of the wick with a set of tweezers and slowly removed it from the wound. Like a multicoloured scarf being pulled from a magician's pocket, the pus-filled wick kept on coming. I cleaned the injury and picked up a fresh wick with a pair of forceps. Holding the wound open, I carefully pushed the forceps into the man's leg, my eyes flicking up to his face as I tried to ascertain how deep the sore penetrated. It wasn't until the forceps were at least three inches inside the man's thigh that he offered a wince.

'Keep going, mate, you can go a bit deeper,' said the Doc.

If I go any deeper I'll be through the other side, I thought.

I pushed until the man flinched again. I then began the tedious process of threading the wick into the wound. When it was done I removed my gloves and took a deep breath. 'That was pretty full-on . . . you're a tough guy,' I said, nodding my head. I didn't bother to ask the

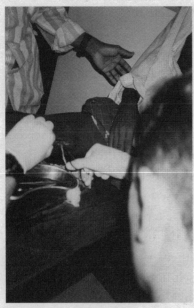

Inserting a sterile wick into a man's leg.

translator to spell it out; the man could see I was impressed.

That day I treated about a dozen patients, from prescribing half an Asprin to thin the blood of a woman with high blood pressure, to treating otitis externa (pus-filled ears), a fungal infection, food allergies and mastitis. The most difficult patient to diagnose suffered from an array of problems: difficulty breathing, swollen feet and clubbing of fingers (thickening of flesh underneath the fingernails). He also had an enlarged liver and spleen.

'It's highly likely this guy has HIV that may have progressed into AIDS, but without a blood test there's no way to be sure,' said the Doc. 'All we can do is treat the symptoms and try to make him feel more comfortable.'

The true extent of HIV on the island was unknown, but according to reports in Dar es Salaam, 60 per cent of all donated blood in the capital was infected with the virus. Because there was no way of determining whether or not someone on Chole Island was HIV positive, it was likely the virus was spreading at an alarming rate. The key was education.

There was one young man who came into the clinic with fluid-filled lungs, a large abdominal tumour and a severe rash over his stomach and lower chest. The lymph glands in his neck, under his arms and in his groin had become so enlarged that two of them had ulcerated the skin and burst.

'Fenno, what's your diagnosis for this guy?'

'By the size of his lymph glands, it looks like he has a major infection,' I said, frantically flicking through my *Patrol Med Aide Memoir.*

'What about the rash?'

I consulted my handbook. 'I don't know . . . it fits the description for herpes.'

'Yeah, it's called herpes zosta. It's a painful rash that can be triggered by a low immune system – a strong indicator that he has AIDS.'

'Can we tell him we think he has AIDS?' I asked.

'No, not without confirmation. I would say he has less than three months to live.'

As I looked at the man, my chest felt heavy. I asked him if I could take his picture, and he smiled and nodded his head. He stood still, his hands by his sides, his head tilted slightly to the right. I have since analysed this photo many times and wondered when it was that he died. My eyes are drawn to the burst lymph node on the left side of his neck. I then look at his eyes, which have the stare of someone who has just died. This man knows something pretty bad is going on inside him.

He would have passed away nearly 10 years ago. To most, he is just another statistic, another African nobody who has succumbed to the virus. But during his

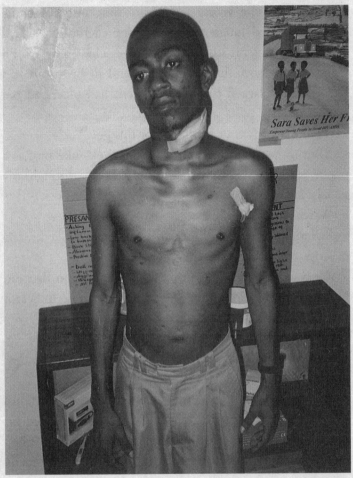

This man knew something pretty bad was going on inside him.

examination, I saw a cheeky side to his persona that I liked. For me, this man was real, as real as death. Sometimes when I think I'm having a shit day I recall this sort of experience, which enables me to put things in their right perspective. A shit day, in reality, is usually still a pretty good day.

That evening, Col and I went for a walk around the island. We climbed through the remains of what appeared to be an old German garrison. Just a few walls remained, swallowed by the forest and covered with vines.

≡

The next morning a man came to the clinic with two puncture wounds on his left ankle. He was in the water when he was bitten by a snake. I immediately applied a pressure immobilisation bandage and informed the Doc.

'Does he feel nauseated or have any stomach cramps?'

'Not that I'm aware of. He looks fine.'

'Then it's probably not poisonous. If it was then there's not a lot we could do. He'd be dead before we got him to the mainland.'

'What, there's no antivenom, not even on Mafia Island?' I asked, almost horrified.

'Nah, mate, depending on the type of snake and the amount of venom, it will either kill him or it won't. Was the wound bleeding?'

'No, it was dry.'

'That's a good sign,' said the Doc. 'Just keep an eye on him and see how he goes.'

I asked the man to wait outside but when I returned he was gone.

Many children on the island were anaemic and had swollen stomachs. We treated them for worms and prescribed Mebendazole. Malaria was also prevalent. We took a blood sample which we analysed under the microscope. Although the Doc explained it several times, I was flat out focusing the thing, let alone making an accurate diagnosis. Children were treated with chloroquinne and liquid paracetamol.

One woman regularly came in complaining of seeing smoke in her eyes. It was bizarre but I think she liked me. Her eyes were fine but she did have high blood pressure. We gave her some tablets to lower her blood pressure. *I'm sure I'll see you in a couple of days*, I thought. She was back the next day.

'I think she likes me.' A woman who complained of smoke-filled eyes.

When I arrived at the centre on 16 January, I saw an elderly man seated in the waiting area. His feet were swollen to an enormous size. *What the freak is going on there?* I thought. The Doc told me the man had elephantiasis. It is caused by a parasite that blocks up the lymphatic system, preventing it from draining.

'If you catch it early, it's reversible,' said the Doc.

'What about this guy?'

'Unfortunately, for him it's too late.'

Running a children's clinic, Chole Island.

It must have been a day for feet, because my next two patients both had deep gashes on their insteps. The first man had been struck by a machete, while the second had had an outboard motor dropped onto his foot. There didn't appear to be any broken bones so we cleaned the wounds and applied steri-strips.

On our second last day the Doc asked if I would like to run a children's clinic.

'Sure,' I said. 'It'll be a good way to finish off.'

Mothers and their babies were lined up all over the place. For them it was a special day, and they'd dressed their babies in their brightest, most flamboyant outfits. They looked gorgeous, but after I'd examined 85 of them I shot Col a look that said: *Is 25 too young to get a vasectomy?*

My initial motivation for wanting to go to Chole Island was two-fold. I hoped to increase my medical knowledge in order to become a better soldier, and I was after adventure. A deep desire to help others really hadn't entered my mind. But after spending a couple of weeks with the Doc and Jackie, their sense of humility and service had a big effect on me.

I'm a believer in the saying 'Hang around what you wish to become'. If you want to be a happy person, stick with people who make you laugh. If you aspire to be a back-stabbing arsehole who never has a good word to say about anyone or anything, then I'm sure there are plenty of people out there who can show you how to get there. The Doc and Jackie were two amazing people who were having an enormous impact on the lives of many. Everyone has goals and dreams for their future, but I don't know too many people who are more driven to help others instead of themselves.

≡

On 23 January Col and I left the island and began our journey north to Arusha. Trying to find the right bus was tough — there were at least 50 jammed in a depot, all parked at different angles with hundreds of people running around yelling. A large African man offered me a challenge.

'Hello, mister, do you box?'

'Do I box,' I said with a smile, as I looked at Col and tried to work out what the guy was on about.

'Yes, boxing. Fitness.'

He began to throw a few punches and dance around.

'Only a little,' I said.

'You look strong. You want to come to boxing gym and train fitness?' He grabbed my upper arm and squeezed it. 'Ooh, very nice!'

Colleen laughed but I knew the guy was serious. He

called over a few of his friends and encouraged them to grab my arm. They were a little less exuberant and just stood there smiling.

'We like fitness and we train very hard,' said the man.

'Yeah, you look fit,' I said.

He flexed his bicep and signalled for me to touch it.

What the hell, we're in Africa, I thought. *If he gets an erection I can always boot him in the balls.* 'We're trying to find the bus for Arusha,' I said.

'Arusha,' he said, excited. 'Come!'

He grabbed my arm and, after a bit of frantic running around, proudly directed us to the right bus.

We thanked him; he smiled, flexed his bicep and left.

We'd paid for three seats – an entire bench seat – but a young African man had squirmed his way between Col and the window. Col looked uncomfortable so she and I traded places. Having the man's sweaty skin pressed against mine was a little irritating.

A woman with a box containing bananas and bottled water tapped on the window.

'How much for two bananas and two bottles of water?' I asked. I had no intention of negotiating; I just wanted to know how many Tanzanian shillings to dig out of my bumbag.

The man next to me took it upon himself to translate and said 3000, the equivalent of US$5. I handed him some money to pass to the woman, and then three bananas and bottles of water were coming our way! The man next to the window kept one of each for himself.

I looked at Col and shrugged my shoulders. *He must have slipped the lady some cash*, I thought. At the next stop

I ordered two ice-creams. Once again, three items were passed back through the window. This time I was laughing. 'How's the hide of this guy?' I said to Col. By the time I had unwrapped my ice-cream, the man had already wiped his lips and thrown his empty stick out the window.

When we arrived at Arusha we were swamped by scores of African men, from overzealous tour guides and hotel workers to men selling local ornaments. I was busy refusing offers when I heard Col scream. I turned around and saw three or four guys with their hands all over her. One was holding a maroon tea towel over her face while another had unzipped her bumbag and was helping himself. I launched into them and sent a couple reeling. I pointed to the man who'd had his hands in her bumbag and told him something that he'd definitely understand: 'You – fuck off!'

He returned the compliment: 'Fucking Americans,' and he walked away.

Col was rattled by the experience so I told her to walk in front of me so I could keep an eye on her. I pulled a map out of my bumbag and we headed off to the YMCA Hotel.

That evening we caught up with Alex and Eliza, friends from Australia who were joining us on a trek up Mount Kilimanjaro. They had flown into Nairobi but had missed their connecting bus to Arusha, so they'd organised a lift with some locals. While squashed in the back of a big black sedan, with several thousand dollars in their pockets, they began to realise how vulnerable they were. There were no streetlights, just a dark road, a car, several men and them – two trusting Aussies.

Eliza is usually pretty controlled but she'd been angry with Alex for their situation, repeatedly referring to him as a 'c—'. She was pissed off that Alex would, most likely, have been killed quickly, leaving her to deal with what followed on her own. She's an attractive young woman and her long, reddish-blonde locks often grab the attention of both men and women. Once a few years earlier when the four of us were in Sydney, a woman handed her a card with a contact number, saying: 'Don't worry, darling, heterosexuality is curable.'

After dinner we relaxed with a couple of drinks. Al and Liz's account of the drive was now hilarious. We sat at a table with a well-dressed African salesman who wore a big shiny watch. I asked him what he sold; I was thinking diamonds.

'Soap,' he said.

'Are you coming to bed,' Col asked me.

'Nah, I think I'll hang around and watch the cricket for half an hour.' Australia was playing South Africa.

'We're out of here,' said Al.

'See you guys tomorrow,' said Liz.

They were barely around the corner when the African man leant over the table and said: 'I think I'll retire too.'

Well, thanks for letting me know, I thought.

Then he dropped his room key into my hand. 'I'm staying in room 16 if you would like to join me.'

I dropped his key on the table and pretended that I didn't understand what he was on about. 'Nah, I'm watching the cricket,' I said, flicking my head back towards the small, fuzzy screen.

'As you wish.' He picked up the key, grabbed his briefcase and calmly left the room.

≡

Early the next morning, from the first floor of the YMCA Hotel, Col and I saw Mount Kilimanjaro for the first time. The ice-capped volcanic rim sat above the clouds, and the round dome glowed in the morning light. We were excited to get going and make it to the top.

With a summit of 19,340 feet – or 5895 metres – above sea level, Kilimanjaro doesn't rate a mention for the serious mountaineer, but of the 30,000 people who attempt to summit it each year, many thousands fail due to a lack of preparation and altitude illness. On average, 10 Western climbers are killed annually on the mountain.

Treks to the north or south base camps of Mount Everest (at 17,600 feet and 17,090 feet respectively) take between 11 and 13 days. To summit Kilimanjaro, depending on the route, budget and tour company you use, only takes between 72 and 96 hours. Trekking from 4000 feet to nearly 20,000 feet in a couple of days is difficult as you

Mount Kilimanjaro from a distance.

have very little time for acclimatisation. Some people are more susceptible to altitude illness than others.

Since joining the Regiment, I had been pushed to the verge of my limitations several times. SAS soldiers must be able to keep going when their body is screaming to stop. But physical fitness and strength will only take you so far. It is the mind – your ability to hold it together when things get really tough – that can give the greatest rewards.

In the weeks before we'd departed Perth, Col had been so excited about the trek that she showed some of her work colleagues a miniature Aussie flag she intended to pull out on the summit.

'Providing you make it to the top, that is,' said a guy named Steve.

Up to that point, Col had assumed that making the summit was a formality. Steve's comments upped the ante for her. She started training even harder, squatting up to 70 kilograms and stomping up and down Jacob's Ladder, a mad set of stairs in central Perth, with a daypack. She also played touch football and worked on her upper-body strength. She could pump out seven chin-ups.

Eliza had also done some training. She and Al had been for a walk the day before they left.

We decided to climb the Machame route; it was steep and a little more expensive, but was regarded as one of the most beautiful routes and would get us away from the masses. There were no huts, though, so we had to hire tents. The locals referred to the Machame as 'Route Whiskey' because it was difficult. One guide and three porters were required per couple.

Alex treks through the rainforest on day one, Mount Kilimanjaro.

The most popular route was the Marangu, or 'Coca-Cola' route, which was slightly longer but far less severe. Dozens of people – up to 70 – travelled the Marangu every day.

We began the trek wearing shorts and T-shirts, as we pulled and stepped our way through a maze of vines and slippery tree roots. The humidity thinned as we negotiated the alpine country, where long grasses, moss and needle-leaf trees replaced the rainforest. We walked approximately 15 kilometres that day, ascending from 6500 feet to 10,000 feet. Camp One was damp and cool.

On day two we left the alpine country and arrived at Shira Hut, a flat rocky plateau sparsely covered with grass and small bushes. We were now perched at 12,500 feet and had covered another nine kilometres. A thick fog had swallowed the mountain.

That night Eliza had a severe headache and began to vomit. I was concerned that she was suffering from altitude illness, but by the following morning both Col and I were also feeling pretty average so it was most likely a stomach bug. I had a word to our guides and asked them to ensure they boiled our drinking water for at least 10 minutes.

Day three was always set aside for acclimatisation, so for most of the day we remained inside our sleeping bags, tucked up in the foetal position, and tried not to shit ourselves. Eliza, Col and I had lost our appetites, so Alex, who was the only one feeling okay, consumed a ridiculous number of hard-boiled eggs.

With each egg he popped into his mouth, he smiled and said: 'Mmm, more protein for me.' I knew eggs and altitude weren't a good mix but I decided to let Al find out for himself. Within a couple of days he too began shooting caramel milkshakes out his arse.

Day four was brilliant. The morning sun was warm, and the air cool and thin. We began climbing again, and by midday there was very little vegetation around us. The landscape was nothing more than rocks and scree. We passed a group of 14 climbers who had established camp at the Lava Tower, a large rocky outcrop that stuck out like a big wart. For most of the day we saw no one else, which was just the way we liked it. We arrived at the base of Arrow Glacier, 16,000 feet above sea level. The late afternoon sun doused the landscape in contrasting shadows. It was cold and beautiful.

'Is anyone keen to walk to the snowline?' I asked. I'd only seen snow a couple of times before and I wanted to touch it.

'Nah, I'm not walking all the way over there,' said Al.

'We'll watch you,' the girls said.

It took me about 20 minutes to reach the base of the cliff. Before I had even touched the ice, I heard a sharp cracking sound followed by distant screams. I didn't bother looking around; the roar of a massive boulder – the size of a small car – bouncing towards me had my undivided attention. I maintained a constant visual as I shuffled to my

A perfect day for trekking on Mount Kilimanjaro.

left. As it gained momentum, the frightening sound of rock slamming into rock intensified. I stopped when I realised I was no longer in its direct path, and I watched it thump by no more than 20 metres to my right.

I stood there a moment and examined the cliffs, my heart beating hard. The weight and speed of that rock was one of the most powerful things I'd ever witnessed. I felt okay so I walked back to the ice and touched it.

Yep, the ice is hard and cold, I thought. *No different from the stuff in the freezer. You're an idiot.*

Access to the summit via the Arrow Glacier was closed for several months in 1996 after three Western climbers were killed by a rockfall. Sometimes people contribute to their own demise, but sometimes, despite the utmost planning and care, Mother Nature just wins out.

We went to bed early as we knew we'd have to set off in the middle of the night. With the sun gone, the temperature had dropped to well below freezing. Col had to go to the toilet, but venturing outside meant throwing on several layers of clothing.

'Just hang your bum outside the tent,' I said. 'There's a fly, so no one will see.'

'You reckon?'

'Yeah, go for it.'

I waited until I heard the trickle of fluid hitting gravel before calling out to one of our guides: 'Hey, Thomas, can you come here, please? Colleen wants to show you something.'

Col was mortified and the casual trickle soon turned into a fire hydrant as she forced the fluid out and dived into her sleeping bag.

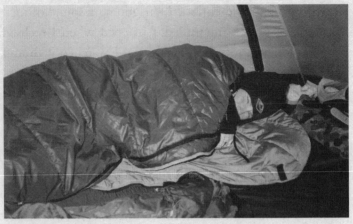

Colleen dived back into her sleeping bag after our guide, Thomas, nearly caught her in a compromising position.

'What's up, Mr Keith?' said Thomas.

'Nothing, Thomas,' said Col. 'Mr Keith's just being an arsehole.'

I laughed and pulled my head inside my sleeping bag.

Throughout the night a strong wind lashed our tents. None of us was able to sleep; I was checking my watch constantly. We rose just after midnight, slowly got dressed and readied our gear. It was cold, but by 0050 we were on our way. We'd been walking for a couple of hours when Col needed a toilet break.

Alex became frustrated because he was cold.

'Why don't you put your Gortex jacket on?' I asked.

'I don't have one.'

'What do you mean? Liz showed me the jacket she bought you – it was perfect.'

'I took it back,' said Al. 'I thought 400 bucks was a waste.'

'You tightarse. Is that all you've got, a $30 spray jacket?'

'Yeah.'

'You dick.'

Al had been sweating underneath his spray jacket, so when we stopped moving he was crippled by the cold. Col was missing, Al and the guides had the shits because they were cold, and Liz was crying because she was afraid of heights. Adventurous holidays with friends and loved ones can be such fun.

I went to look for Col so we could get going. Not knowing that she had diarrhoea and stomach cramps, she took offence with my tone and lashed out with a left. I offered her a drink of water but my camelback hydration pack was frozen. We laughed and shared a Mars Bar instead.

From that point on, Col set a cracking pace. Despite the thin air, she was powering up the mountain. By 0515 we had reached a plateau and began skirting around a large glacier. Al and Liz had been suffering from altitude illness for a couple of hours and both had severe headaches. As we scaled the final 200 metres, my brain also felt like it was being cut in half.

By the time we reached 19,000 feet, all of us except for Col were dizzy. We could only walk 20 to 30 paces before having to sit down. My heart was pounding as if I had just completed a running race, and our lungs had to suck hard for air. There never seemed to be enough oxygen to go around. The air was cold, the coldest my lungs had ever inhaled. The guides said it was somewhere between −15 and −17 degrees Celsius.

As we approached the summit, Col started jumping up and down. *Where in the hell is all this excess energy coming from?* I wondered. To our right was a thick glacial wall rising above a frozen body of water. To our left was a brown box with three metal poles jutting out of the top. The rock beneath our feet was uneven but not slippery.

As we got closer we noticed the box was covered with stickers. There was also a brown piece of timber, a metre

Colleen as the highest person in Africa.

long and 20 centimetres wide. Carved into the wood in yellow letters were the words: *YOU ARE NOW AT THE UHURU PEAK, THE HIGHEST POINT IN AFRICA. ALTITUDE 5895 METRES A.S.L.*

It was a euphoric moment, and we were the first to summit that day. No one was more excited than Colleen. She had trained hard and was ecstatic to have achieved her goal. In fact, she was so excited that she insisted that she sit on my shoulders and get a photo – proof that she was, at that moment, the highest person in Africa.

10

PHYSICAL TRAINING

Six months after joining an SAS sabre squadron, I was given the task of coordinating the physical training (PT) for a troop of 20 SAS soldiers. I was offered this task during my first year in the troop because of my passion for physical fitness.

Intense physical training has always been an integral part of my life. When I'm training hard, I feel there's nothing in life that I cannot achieve. I feel in control, in charge of my own destiny – proactive, rather than reactive. The endorphin rush that comes from an arduous workout gives me an addictive natural high that I would struggle to live without. It makes me feel alive. My senses sharpen and life's stresses become less significant. They don't disappear, but they are re-categorised – refiled in order of their real priority.

Running the PT for a troop of SAS soldiers was hardly a challenge, as all the guys were highly motivated – many already were at an elite level of fitness. My job was to ensure we achieved a balance between cardiovascular fitness, strength and endurance, and that the sessions were controlled; in an SAS water troop, where alpha males dominate, physical training could easily become a testosterone-charged dick-pulling contest. In writing this, however, I know I've been guilty of running my fair share of sessions like that, especially during my first couple of years in the troop.

=

Seeing the way my three children approach exercise takes me back to the type of child I was growing up. Children are motivated by what they see and hear, but if a child has no interest or desire to do something, then it's not going to happen. Our eldest daughter, Tahlie, who is eight, often rises early, throws on her swimmers and a jumper and sits next to the garage door in the dark to ensure I don't leave for a session down at the beach without her. When she was seven she conned me into letting her paddle her nipper

Tahlie doing what she loves most: catching waves on her paddle board.

board from our local beach to a distant headland – a return trip of 3.5 kilometres. Colleen wasn't happy and said, 'If she doesn't come back then it's probably best that you don't either.'

The journey saw us negotiate some deep sections of water about 500 metres from the coast. On the way back I noticed that a lot of the time Tahlie's forehead was nestled on the front of her board – her neck wasn't strong enough to cope with the demands of such a long paddle. At one stage she peered at me through her stringy fringe and I saw that her forehead was chafed. I smiled to myself. *Bet you won't be bugging me to do this again for a while*, I thought.

What came out of her mouth surprised me: 'Dad, can we do this every Sunday?'

Her younger sister, Sian, aged seven, is no different. When she was six we went for a jog; I was thinking she'd be content with a couple of laps around the oval. After the first lap she told me we'd be doing it 20 times. And as for our son, Reyne, who has recently turned five: he's yet to start school but has asked his mum, Colleen, if she will train him for the school cross-country races.

So when did my passion for training begin? My parents weren't really into it. Ma played tennis and Dad played a little touch football. He also curled a piece of steel he kept in the garage, which gave him a set of arms that intimidated all my friends. I was probably nine or 10 years old when I told my organ teacher about an impending sports carnival. He was a young guy who didn't care about teaching music, and I was a kid who had potential but didn't wish to learn – perfect! Our 30-minute session was usually filled with him talking about girls and cars while I played

'Can we go for a run, Dad?'

a song or two. I told him that I wanted to beat a guy called Jamie in the 100-metre sprint as I was sick of coming second. He told me I needed to do sprints on the road to strengthen my legs.

The next day I rose early, threw on a pair of sneakers that probably had very little padding, and sprinted up and down the road, from lightpole to lightpole. Apparently, my shoes slapping against the bitumen made quite a racket as my neighbours soon asked my parents what I was doing. Not one to do anything in moderation, and having no clue about recovery, I pounded the asphalt every day for a couple of weeks.

After smoking Jamie, I ran to my ma, who was watching from the hill, and blurted out: 'Mum, I did it! I beat Jamie!'

Her face instantly changed colour. 'Keith, this is Jamie's mum . . .'

Then my face changed colour. Although I'd beaten him, the poor bastard had been suffering from a chest cold so shouldn't even have been running. At the time I attributed the victory to my preparation on the road, rather than acknowledging the wheezing chest of my adversary. Nevertheless, this is one of the earliest memories I have of setting a goal and following through.

About a year after that I started martial arts. As I progressed through the belts, my interest and enthusiasm began to soar. My taekwondo instructor, Charlie, was a good man who took a keen interest in my progression. I didn't have any more natural ability than my friends, but Charlie identified in me a sense of determination like his own. I would rarely miss a class, which is something that I have maintained to this very day – consistency. I refuse to let things such as the weather dictate how or when I train.

My general fitness level has barely changed over the last 15 years. Besides spiking for the occasional event, I maintain a regular and diverse training program – a sound base to launch from – because it is far less violent on the body and minimises injury and illness. My most severe injury – a knee reconstruction – was the result of overtraining and fatigue after a deployment overseas.

By age 13 I had decided to commit the next 12 months of my life to preparing for my black belt in taekwondo. Physically, I would be expected to perform the same board breaks as men who were aged in their twenties and thirties. Weighing in at less than 50 kilograms, I couldn't rely on brute strength or body mass, so I worked on my speed and technique. I regularly began to kick the back of the house, leaving grimy heel-marks all over the white bricks. Besides the noise, Dad gave me a serve for soiling the bricks and said I would crack the house, so I moved to the barbecue area and continued to slam the wall there. This lasted a day before Dad brought home half a dozen car tyres, sliced them down one side and looped them around a tree near the railway line at the back of the house.

After achieving a black belt in taekwondo I soon became restless. I wanted to study something more effective, so I began wing chun kung-fu. At age 16 I was driving my shins into those tyres most afternoons, only stopping when the bruises, welts and cuts made it too painful to train. I probably would have been well suited to hanging out in a monastery with a shaved head and an orange robe, and training seven days a week.

A year later I was preparing for my wing chun level one instructor grading – black belt equivalent – when I decided to vary my training to enhance my fitness. I included a couple of weekly circuits at the gym. At 17, after passing my grading, I was running my own kung-fu branch twice a week, and travelling to Sydney three times a week for my own training. I also used to get together with a few mates and spar two or three times a week.

I maintained this demented level of intensity until I was 19, when my enthusiasm began to fade. I was hoping to join the police force, so I began resistance training in order to put on a few kilograms. I gave up martial arts a year later – I was burnt out – to concentrate on weights training and general fitness.

My occupation as a motor mechanic was beginning to wear thin. In fact, it was driving me insane. I wanted a job that was exciting, and where I would be challenged. Each morning I struggled to get out of bed; the thought of putting a van on the hoist, dropping the oil, changing the spark plugs and painting the tyres made me want to pick a fight with my father in the hope he would put me out of my misery and sack me. My old man was an excellent mechanic. I was flat-out just popping the bonnet. I put all of my hopes on making it into the police force, but when I found out there was a 12-month freeze on applications, I decided to look elsewhere.

In the Regiment, from the second I opened my eyes my body became excited with the thought of going to work. Not everything we did in the Regiment was exhilarating – I'd rather mow the lawns than wash boats, de-service engines or clean weapons, as that was too much like a mechanic's work for me. But in nine years I never felt like rolling over and taking the day off – never! I would rise from bed, do the obvious, get dressed and have something to eat. My heart rate would be slightly elevated as I thought about the physical training session that would begin at 0745.

When employed as a motor mechanic, I probably never arrived 10 minutes early; I usually scurried in the door at the same time the radio announcer said it was 8 am. I wouldn't look at Dad – there was no point. I could feel his frustration burning holes in my back as I slipped on my boots. Sometimes he'd tap his watch, other times he'd look at the spark-plug clock before glaring in my direction. *Give me a break*, I thought. *I'm stuck here for the next eight hours, so there's no way I'm getting here any earlier than I have to.*

In the Regiment, if I wasn't seated in the troop office gobbing off at least 15 or 20 minutes early, then something was wrong. I was never late, but on one occasion it was close.

I pulled up at a set of lights on a Kawasaki ZXR 750 motorbike wearing the usual: a pair of rugby shorts, a

T-shirt and joggers. My reluctance to wear appropriate attire was the reason I eventually sold the bike. At the lights a white Commodore pulled up alongside me and revved its engine. Underneath my visor I just rolled my eyes and didn't even bother looking at the guy. *What a goose*, I thought. The light turned green and I accelerated up the hill.

After 400 metres, I checked my rear-vision mirror and was surprised to see the Commodore having a real go. Rather than letting him drive past, I kicked down a couple of gears and accelerated hard. As my bike revved through the power band I looked in my mirror and felt satisfied – I had opened up a 100-metre lead. However, this ceased when I saw a blue light flashing through the windscreen. *Shit!* I pulled over, got off my bike and removed my helmet. I had no idea how fast I was going.

'Have you even got a license for that thing,' yelled the officer.

I nodded and presented my motorbike license, which was snatched from my hand.

'You better have a bloody good reason for riding like that.'

'I am running a little late, but that's not why I accelerated up the hill,' I said.

Bip, bip, bip, bip sounded a horn as one of the SAS boys drove past. I didn't wave.

'Where do you work?' the officer asked.

'Swanbourne,' I said.

'Campbell Barracks?'

'Yes.'

The officer returned my license. 'Slow down, mate,' he

said. 'Next time, if someone pulls up alongside and revs their car then at least take the time to have a look. It may also be worth throwing on a pair of jeans and a jacket. If you do come off there'll be nothing left of you.'

I've owned several motorbikes, and I did many irresponsible things between the ages of 17 and 21. That sudden rush of blood can change your life in an instant. Many young men feel invincible and have little thought of self-preservation. This is an attitude that diminishes with age, although I still struggle with it. My mother never attempted to talk me out of buying a motorbike as she knew it'd be futile to try. Instead, she sent a top-of-the-range Shoei helmet to me in Perth.

So how should we encourage young males to drive or ride in a sensible manner? This is a challenge I'm sure I will be confronted with when my son, Reyne, turns 17. For me, the most effective motivation is to make a young man aware not of what he might do to himself, but of how his actions might impact on others. The more graphic television advertisements in which young men drive recklessly and kill innocent people have had a far greater effect on me than the doubling of fines did. And if that doesn't work, then I'll buy Reyne a clapped-out Datsun and remove a spark plug or two.

≡

For SAS soldiers, having a high level of physical fitness, strength and endurance is not simply desirable; it is essential for our very survival. My experiences in the Regiment taught me that. From scrambling up the side of a mountain in Afghanistan, to trying to control our breathing while being hunted by militia forces in East Timor, to negotiating heavy seas while diving from oil platforms – the fitter and stronger the soldier, the greater his contribution to the team.

In the Regiment I rarely felt the need to look for excitement after I knocked off. It was the perfect job for someone with my personality. We were taught how to drive correctly, from seating and hand positions and vehicle dynamics, to braking, steering, cornering and acceleration skills. The training took place under stringent safety procedures at forgiving locations, such as racetracks and skidpans. I had no need to find a dirt road on my time off and throw a car sideways. Then there was the parachuting, climbing, roping, working with explosives, shooting and diving. We were also challenged intellectually, with medical, language, signals and computer skills. It was a brilliant combination that met our intellectual and physical desires.

As good as the specialist training was, I still looked forward to our morning PT sessions the most. On Monday mornings we would run the cross-country, an eight-kilometre soft-sand run. We'd slow-jog to the range sentry gate before stretching. At this stage there was usually still some talking, but most guys would fall silent as they began to psyche themselves up for the run.

If I was coordinating the session, I would attempt to control the speed until we reached the pumphouse near the beach. Trying to restrain 15 or 20 competitive guys who were keen to unleash was always difficult. We all wanted to be at the front. After reaching the pumphouse we would slow-jog along an orange gravel track before hitting the most challenging section of the course — two kilometres of sand dunes.

Not even a medic with an unlimited supply of valium-charged syringes would be able to calm the guys down from this point on. It simply became a race. The troop was so competitive that it was rare for any one person to dominate. If the guy in front maintained a cracking pace, then the next three or four guys would make use of his footsteps and wait for their own chances to pounce. If Kane, Charlie, Mick or the Boss led the pack, then that chance may never come. However, if a pretender — someone who had let his ambitions get ahead of his ability — tried to sneak into the lead — he might hear something like 'Knew you'd fade, pussy!' as a group of up to half a dozen men churned up the sand around him.

The lead pack would run hard but just within their limits, holding back a little for the monster sand dune known as 'the bowl'. At the top of each hill we would try to maintain our stride — quite a feat when your legs are heavy and burning with lactic acid. Our lungs fared no better. The front group would remain tight until the track swung west into the bowl. No one paced himself from here on in. Quite often it would be Kane who took the lead through the lower bowl, with the rest of us jostling for position. Then it was on. The gradient was perfect — steep. Kane would always go hard early but we'd often claw him back with five metres to go. He sometimes held on to win, but any one of three or four guys would hit the summit within half a metre of each other.

We'd then jog back to the rear gate, although sometimes this would become a second race.

Many guys would do their own strength work in the afternoons, so the morning PT sessions were a mix of running, swimming and circuit-training. A Tuesday might include a boxing circuit, or the guys might grab a 17-kilogram pipe and spend an hour curling, pressing and squatting the thing. We usually worked in pairs; one man would do 50 bicep curls before handing the bar to his partner. The second set would be 40 reps, followed by 30, 20 and then 10. With this complete, we'd pyramid back up to 50. The last two sets usually aroused a little grunting, as the guys maintained a balance between good form and racing each other.

A typical Wednesday included a transition session in the pool. It would begin with a 300-metre swim followed by a one-kilometre run. Without resting, the guys would then complete swims of 250, 200, 150, 100 and 50 metres, each separated by another one-kilometre run. This is a fantastic way to train. Just as the body begins to find a rhythm, it's thrust into a contrasting activity. Your blood is shunted from your legs to your upper torso. These sessions slightly favoured runners over swimmers.

A pool session often concluded with some underwater work to boost lung capacity. Everyone in the water troop had to be capable of swimming 25 metres underwater. The top guys, when fresh, could push double this – up to 60 metres. Carrying out a 'free ascent' – swimming from a tie-off line to a target vessel or oil platform with a single breath – always turned me on. I loved the challenge of trying to swim underneath a ship, especially in dark or murky conditions.

I've since taken an interest in breath-hold training and

am blown away by what some free-divers are able to achieve.

I realised the importance of remaining calm under-water when I lost my board in eight- to 10-foot storm swell and was caught in the impact zone. Sucked to the bottom over and over again, I had to force myself to remain calm.

'Static apnea' is an underwater discipline that requires a participant to hold their breath for as long as possible while their face remains underwater. After my first couple of attempts I managed three minutes and 10 seconds. I increased my preparation time, and four weeks later I held my breath for five minutes. I thought this was okay until

Underwater training: a 55-metre run, carrying two 32-kilogram kettlebells.

I viewed footage of a French guy holding his breath for 10 minutes.

With just a few weeks training, my lungs seemed stronger and more efficient. I don't do a lot of running – one track session and a mountain run each week – but within three weeks I had lowered my one-kilometre track time by 20 seconds.

The guys I train in the ocean with – Chris, Perry and Brett – are hard chargers who are also keen to increase their lung capacity. We began breath-hold training in a sand-bottom ocean pool. While carrying two 32 kilogram kettle-bells, we'd run 55 metres underwater. Running with a combined weight of 64 kilograms sees our lungs scream-ing for air before we're even halfway. To push the entire length of the pool and beyond is mentally and physically challenging. To work our upper bodies, we pull ourselves along a rope that is secured with kettle-bells to the bottom of the pool. Within a couple of sessions we were able to make 90 metres with a single breath. After 90 metres, I'd return to the surface dizzy and then float on my back as my lungs suck hard for air. I noticed that Chris was standing beside me, ready to pluck me out of the water if I pushed it a little too far.

Underwater training is dangerous and can be unforgiv-ing. If someone panics or extends beyond their limits, there is a chance they can experience an underwater blackout. The training must be controlled and never performed alone. I always take the time to give a safety brief, which covers actions on something going wrong.

When we're finished I usually run a modified session for our children, who are eager to dive to the bottom and pull their way along the rope. It's great for their water confidence. On a recent trip in the car, Tahlie's best friend, Kate, asked me a question: 'Keith, are we doing breath-hold training tomorrow?' A nine-year-old girl enquiring about breath-hold training sounded tough. I looked at Colleen and we both laughed.

Underwater training: a 90-metre rope traverse.

Sometimes I run sessions in rivers. I had the opportunity to train three hard-hitting corporate clients. By the end of the session each person was dragging a 24-kilogram kettle-bell across the bottom of a sandy river. To take a breath, they had to make it the 10 metres to the other side. Considering that one of these people wasn't comfortable in water, it was an amazing effort. I took as much inspiration out of the session as they did.

Another exercise I do with non-military clients is to put a set of blacked-out goggles on one person and have another person guide them out the back of a surf zone without touching them. It is an excellent activity for communication and trust. You have to be clear and concise with your commands. This activity is dependent on surf conditions and one's ability.

I also sometimes conducted an exercise that I learnt from the US Navy Seals. If the participant is confident enough, he or she wears a blacked-out set of goggles and has their hands restrained behind their back with a thick elastic band. In a pool with a depth of at least 2.5 metres, you have to sink your body by exhaling quickly and firmly. When your feet touch the bottom, you crouch and drive towards the surface. Once your head breaks the surface, naturally, you take a breath. Then you repeat the exercise any given number of times. Someone who is uncomfortable might only manage five repetitions, while a person who is fit and confident can continue for several minutes. If you don't blow the air out quickly enough, you'll sink too slowly, or you might only sink a foot or two, and so you have to kick to reach the surface. If you're tentative when driving off the bottom then you'll also have to kick to the surface, burning up valuable oxygen. This type of training is hugely beneficial for confidence in the water, and over time it will give you a set of lungs like a whale.

≡

Depending on the intensity of our previous three sessions, on Thursdays we would often do an interval session. This could include five one-kilometre sprints, fartlek training or – my last troop sergeant's favourite – the seven peaks.

We used to jog around Swanbourne and, every few minutes, select a hill and race to the top. The winner would receive gold, second place silver and bronze for third. The others were given a bowl of milk and told to try a little harder. The key to this was making your efforts at the right time. You shouldn't give 100 per cent on every hill, but rather decide when to go for it and when to conserve your energy. No one ever won two hills in a row. At the end of the session, the person with the most gold, silver and bronze was the winner. There was no second place – just 19 losers.

During those sessions there was always a lot of banter. On one occasion a strong sprinter and road-runner named Charlie said: 'Hey, let's all work together so Fenno doesn't get any gold medals.'

Why single me out, ya' bastard? I thought. I waited for the second sprint and yelled out: 'Fuck you, Charlie!' before taking off on my quest for gold.

Training hard together builds an esprit de corps. We were tight, a critical constituent for soldiers who might be sent to war at any time.

On Saturday mornings a few of us would meet at the Regimental gymnasium. Once a month we would go berserk and shock-load our bodies to test ourselves. Kane and I used to do a heavy chin-up/push-up session – 300 of each in 30 minutes. When Newy, a mate from another troop, heard about this, he asked to join in. We decided to up the ante to 400 chin-ups and 400 push-ups in 45 minutes. At the start of each minute we'd jump onto the heave bar and pump out 10 chin-ups. As soon as we were finished that we'd drop to the floor for 10 push-ups. This would have taken around 22 to 25 seconds, and we'd use the remainder of that minute to rest. After 30 continuous sets we would stop for a two-minute break.

'What do you think, Newy – you like it?' I asked at the break, trying not to laugh.

'It's a cracker! You fuckers are sick!'

Newy was a hyper-positive soldier who radiated energy. If someone was having a bad day, all they'd have to do was spend 10 minutes with Newy – then they'd be bouncing off the walls like he was, feeling stoked to be alive. He had a witty sense of humour and would often crack one-liners that Raymond Chandler would be proud of. He was also tall, exceptionally fit and one of the strongest swimmers in the Regiment. Kane and I looked forward to hurting Newy.

We completed another five sets before taking a further minute to rest. Our backs were beginning to cramp. Newy and his long arms were still hanging in there, but only just.

'Five sets to go, big guy,' I said.

'Is that all,' he said, bending over and shaking his arms.

After 350 chin-ups and push-ups, our arms felt like they were going to burst. We rested after sets 37 and 39. On the penultimate set, our form had well and truly gone to shit. We flicked our hips like a dog having sex as we tried to get our chins over the bar. Just hanging on was an effort.

'Good effort, boys,' said Kane.

'Yeah, thanks for that, fellas,' said Newy. 'If my arms weren't so useless I'd punch you both in the face.' He slumped down on the bench.

A few weeks later it was Buzz's turn. He was my first team leader and always keen for a challenging hit-out. The aim of the session was to complete five consecutive exercises without a rest, before taking a 90-second break and repeating the whole thing another four times. The first exercise was 10 chin-ups with a 10-kilogram plate slung around our waists. Then we'd jump onto the bench press and pump out 20 repetitions of 60 kilograms. From there we'd walk to the squat rack and complete 20 deep squats with 60 to 80 kilograms, before completing another 10 chin-ups and finishing off with 30 push-ups.

The first set is okay – you finish feeling pumped and your heart is beating hard. The second set starts to bite. By the third, you start to doubt whether there is enough blood and oxygen in your body to get the job done. During the fourth set, your body gets a little freaked out – a combination of rising nausea and dizziness – as you struggle to complete the reps. During our final 90-second rest, no one was talking and no one was sitting. We were all collapsed on the benches or the floor, hyperventilating and trying to summon the courage for the final set.

The chin-ups are a rest compared to the bench press, which is the most challenging activity. For me, the final two reps of the fifth set are always a struggle. The final trip to the squat bar is like trying to walk in a straight line after you have spun around 10 times with your eyes closed. If you're not dizzy when you start the squats, you might well be hallucinating by the time you get off. Then it's back on the chin-up bar before pumping out one final set of push-ups.

Buzz finished the workout – with no build-up training, we were impressed that he completed all the reps – then he walked outside and fertilised the garden. Now that's what we were hoping for.

≡

Despite this type of training, trying to pull yourself out of a violent, windswept ocean in Bass Strait while burdened with 15 to 20 kilograms of equipment – body armour, a climbing harness, safety vest, weapons, ammunition, a radio and a sledge hammer – is still hugely taxing. After completing a dive and establishing a 30- to 40-foot caving ladder, the final climb is always gruelling as blood is shunted between your legs and arms. If the water is cold — and it always is — then even hanging on to the ladder can be challenging.

The same goes for trying to remain coherent when scrambling up the side of a mountain in Afghanistan while carrying in excess of 65 kilograms.

The years we spent physically preparing and extending ourselves in training allowed us to perform during exacting operational deployments. In the SAS, being physically fit and strong is not about ego; it's about being able to get the job done and embrace tasks that are beyond the scope and capabilities of conventional military units.

It's different now. I no longer train for survival, but for sanity and enjoyment.

Although I consume a fairly balanced diet (one that does include pizza, Diet Coke and chocolate), my love of training does not extend to excessive protein consumption, which can trigger more than one sitting on a toilet per day, or to counting calories, hanging out in front of the mirror or balancing on scales. I like to train hard primarily because of how it makes me feel.

For the most part, I enjoy training with other like-minded people, but when I need to get back to basics, gather my inner thoughts and centre myself — as I did after SAS selection — I train alone. Taking on a heavy, wind-battered ocean; having a rigorous session on the kettlebells; or running up a densely wooded mountain, where I have nothing but the sound of my own laboured breathing to keep me company — these activities strengthen my soul.

They enhance my self-belief, as during those times I have no safety net. The only person I have for motivation – the only person I can rely on – is me.

Going solo against nature is as humbling as it is invigorating, and in more ways than purely the physical. The mental strength that enables you to conquer an extreme workout can be carried over to all other facets of life. For me, it's simple; a testing workout builds my self-esteem and self-belief, but also keeps my feet on the ground and promotes humility.

These days, I do most of my training in the ocean with a few mates, and I've started competing for our local surf

A mountain workout.

club. My whole family is into it too. Having the time to train for an event, and then actually being around long enough to go in it, has opened up my eyes to life after the Regiment. It was always there but it took me a while to find it. I've also met some remarkable people. When I first started training on a paddle board, an elderly gentlemen named Ross would regularly kick my arse. I'm 35 and he's 64; he's not double my age but he's close enough. This man and several others like him are inspirational.

≡

The fourteenth of January 2009 started off a little more exciting than most days. I arrived at the beach at 0600. The sun was not yet fully round, its arse still below the horizon. There was a slight breeze out of the north-west. *Excellent – the winds are offshore*, I thought.

I said g'day to Chris, a mad surfer mate who, like me, is now addicted to intense training on racing paddle-boards. I've met a great crew of guys who don't mind training hard. On this day, there were just three of us – Chris, myself and Brendon, a tenacious older guy in his mid to late forties. We decided to paddle 1000 metres around the rocks to the next beach, where we completed some beach and pool sprints before heading back. We'd been training for 50 minutes, so I decided to conclude the session with some interval training.

We consolidated at a buoy about 150 metres from the shore, where I explained to the guys how it would work. The aim of the training was to work through the phosphate and into the lactic acid energy system. In simple terms, we'd paddle hard around an opposite buoy in 45-second bursts – flat-out – to develop our power and speed. Since there were three of us, while one man was paddling the other two would rest. I normally prefer 1:1 rest when doing interval training, but the additional time off meant we could pull ourselves through the water a little harder.

'This will be the last one, mate,' I said to Chris, angling my board towards the buoy, waiting for Brendon to arrive back. He, as usual, was throwing his heart and soul into the session. When he was 10 metres away I began paddling towards him. I grabbed my side rails and prepared to jump onto my knees and get going, but a second later I noticed a large black shape breach the swell about three metres behind him. There was a distinctive wake, and the shape – the shark's head – was heading straight towards him, its speed at least double his. It's well known that sharks generally attack from below or behind.

It was bizarre. Before me was a perfect demonstration of a shark's final approach before an attack. Brendon was two or three metres from me when the head sank beneath the water. It turned right, revealing a shadow of considerable girth and at least three metres long.

Brendon's board glided past mine as I said: 'Oy, guys, there's something in the water, and it's fucking big.'

Brendon, who should by then have been recovering and enjoying his well-deserved rest, spun around towards Chris, his flushed face redder than his hair. Some people might have been overwhelmed by the thought of something big feasting on their body, and filled with panic. But these guys were the complete opposite – I was impressed.

'Hey, hold on, Keith saw something in the water,' said Chris.

'It had a bloody big head,' I said as we lay on our boards – with none of our appendages dangling in the water. We signalled to a dozen surfers 60 metres up the beach, then cautiously paddled up to them to spread the word.

'Guys, we're not trying to freak anyone out, but a decent-sized shark surged towards one of our boards. It was big. Just wanted to let you know.'

'Cheers, mate,' one said. They were cool. Some guys stayed, some paddled in.

I've read that sharks have no apprehension about approaching something if they are twice its size. Perhaps that's why this one didn't follow through. It was lining up the back of Brendon's board when it would have sensed two other shadows – Chris and I – moving its way. I guess it didn't expect that. Either that or, as Brendon said, it changed its mind when it noticed that he was a ranga – a redhead – and that his white legs were a little too raw for consumption.

On the beach, a fisherman told me that he was out there last week in a 22-foot boat when a 15-foot great white shark came alongside for a look.

'Yeah, they're out there,' I said.

'Sure are – it's where they live,' he replied.

I returned home and was met by Tahlie and one of her equally impatient friends, Kate. 'Dad, how was the surf – is it big?'

'Nah, it's just okay,' I replied.

'Can we go now?' asked Tahlie.

During the summer holidays, I usually run a bit of training for the children who are competing at the NSW Surf Life Saving state titles. The kids are amazing. At just eight or nine years of age they have already developed a deep love of the ocean. Depending on the conditions, they usually paddle around the buoy half a dozen times and then finish off with a few waves.

At 0800 we were back down at the beach. Bob, Kate's dad, sent the dozen or so kids on a warm-up run while I told their parents about what I'd seen. No one was too concerned, but we ran a modified session. Chris volunteered to hang out the back on a rescue board and provided water safety while the kids practised ins and outs in the surf zone. At the end of the session, a few of the kids hung around to catch waves. Jake, a keen 14-year-old, asked if he could paddle out the back.

'If you want – just be careful,' I said.

'You coming?' he asked. 'You don't have to.'

I laughed. I knew there was something I liked about this kid.

'Yeah, I'll come with ya.' Chris and I joined him out the back and caught a few waves.

'Hey, Chris,' I said. 'We never did finish that session. We've still got one more to go. Can't let a shark interfere with our training – gotta get back on the horse!' I said.

'Yeah, we do. No point delaying it,' replied Chris, grinning.

Although I was a little apprehensive, I was determined to get back out to the buoy as soon as possible. It had been two hours since the incident. *That's long enough*, I thought. The three of us paddled to the buoy, had a look around, then paddled back in.

'You training Friday?' asked Chris.

'Yeah, same time. See you then.'

We thought that would be the end of it, but later that day someone called the local paper and I was invited down to the beach for an interview.

'Look, nothing really happened,' I said over the phone. 'A large head broached the surface next to a few of us and an hour later we were down there with the kids.' I declined to do an interview because I didn't want to add to the exaggerated media frenzy and discourage people from enjoying the ocean.

The next day, on the front page of the local paper was a picture of a great white leaping out of the water. The story was titled 'Thirroul Surfers' Close Encounter: Great White Shark Scare'. All of a sudden, the story read, a '3.5 metre white pointer menaced surfers . . . [and] flashed its pearly whites.' The beach was also 'cleared within minutes'.

I hadn't seen any teeth, and half a dozen surfers continued to catch waves. Now that's quality investigative journalism. I was also quoted as saying: 'It sort of jumped out of the water right next to one of the guys, had a look around and then dived down and swam off.' My nan picked up the paper, read the article and nearly had a heart attack when she saw my name.

Although the article was an extreme example of poetic license – in other words, bullshit – I was impressed by how Chris and Brendon remained calm after we learned about what was lurking beneath us. For me, and obviously for them, fear of letting our mates down well surpassed our fear of being eaten.

≡

Life in the SAS was both mentally and physically challenging. I thrived on this combination. I also knew that my
decision to leave such a lifestyle so I could be a dad had
left me vulnerable; I missed the camaraderie, the action
and the intellectual stimulation. If I was to have any
chance of breaking away, it was vital that I looked forward
and set myself new challenges.

11

DEALING WITH TRANSITION

Very little, if anything, that lives lasts forever. In some ways it would be nice to know the precise moment when we will draw our last breath. Armed with this knowledge, we might well get on with living, rather than thinking about what was, or what could have been.

When I was employed as a special-operations advisor in the United Arab Emirates, my boss, a former British special-forces soldier, offered some advice when he realised I was struggling with my transition away from the Regiment.

'Keith, we all think about going back. Most guys struggle for at least two years, but I think it'll take you three.'

In fact even he was wrong. For almost six years I wrestled with thoughts of returning to the Regiment. Even in the two years since leaving the private security industry, I've battled hard to remain at home. I missed the camaraderie, the rush of adrenaline and that feeling you get when you're being challenged under extreme conditions. When job offers arrived, I often deleted the emails without opening them, so as to not be tempted back into the fray.

I didn't trust myself, so I kept busy writing, studying, training and looking after our three children.

When SAS soldiers leave the Regiment – often to spend more time with family or to seek new challenges – they usually feel as if life has lost its spark. You wake up in the morning and, for the first time in years, struggle to crawl out of bed. Even for those who are gainfully employed, their new jobs just don't cut it compared to life in the Regiment. It takes time for a soldier to detune, to wind down and to appreciate the other things life has to offer.

These are normal feelings that many people experience. When professional athletes retire, when mothers or fathers take time out to raise their children or when people leave the workforce, there is always a period of transition that they must negotiate. Leaving something that you're good at is difficult. You might have thoughts – insecurities – that you'll never reach that level of achievement again. Walking away can be an even greater challenge than getting there in the first place. Initially, there is a void, a chasm so deep and so wide that constructing a bridge over it to a new life seems impossible.

After I gave an interview last year following publication of *Warrior Brothers*, a psychologist approached me and said: 'Keith, after listening to some of your experiences, I must say that you sound surprisingly normal.'

I laughed. *You really have no idea*, I thought. He asked me if I'd ever received professional counselling, as he dealt with many former special-forces soldiers who were finding the transition to a civilian lifestyle unbearable.

'No, I haven't,' I said.

'That's interesting. Many soldiers who experience

combat are wound super-tight. They wake up in the middle of the night with elevated pulse rates. With no release, they struggle to come back down. I would like to know how you did it.'

'Writing my book was cathartic,' I said, 'but it was the new challenges and intense training sessions that kept me grounded when I was vulnerable to that. I'd sometimes grab a piece of paper and write down what I most wanted out of life. Having a relationship with my kids was right up there, and I set about making sure that happened. I think the attributes that helped me to get into the Regiment were the same ones that helped me to walk away. I also realised that, first and foremost, I was a person, a man. I didn't define myself by my job title.'

'What do you mean?' asked the psychologist.

'Well, being an SAS soldier was what I did for a job. To be honest, it was more than that – it was a lifestyle. But just because I left the SAS, it didn't mean that I was anything less than what I was. For example, if you're a company CEO and you define yourself by your position, you could struggle with a loss of identity when you leave the job. It's the same for a sports star. I wouldn't call Roger Federer simply a tennis star – he's much more than that. He's a man with strengths and weaknesses. He's a man who is committed and has worked hard to become one of the best tennis players in history. But if he didn't play tennis, then he most likely would have excelled at something else.'

'That's true, Keith, but negotiating the middle ground, from one life to another, is where most people struggle.'

'I think it's where everyone struggles. I had to set myself new and realistic goals. I had to concentrate on where I wanted to go rather than where I had been. But I still find it difficult.'

≡

For me, a divided loyalty is a hell of a thing to live with. Leaving my family for an operational deployment always felt similar to not being there with the boys when they suffered casualties. The latter has an even greater effect on me.

Colleen and I had every intention of returning to Perth for the Regiment's fiftieth anniversary celebrations in 2007. We had even booked our flights, but I didn't get on the plane. I knew it was still too early to go back. If I caught up with the boys and heard their stories, then the chances were good that I'd be straight back in. But I'd also be single and the next time I took a breath I'd be 40, maybe even 50. At best I'd have a mediocre relationship with my children, as I have an 'all or nothing' personality. If you're a former alcoholic, there's no such thing as drinking in moderation. It's the same for a soldier. To perform, I would have to throw myself into the job with total commitment. Total commitment would mean my family once again came second. It was time to move on.

How does one transition from an adrenalised lifestyle as an SAS soldier and security contractor, working in some of the world's most hostile locations, to a life as a husband and home dad?

I left the SAS in 2002 and moved with my family to the United Arab Emirates, where I was employed as a special-operations advisor. With no chance of being deployed, I felt like a young man in an old man's job. Most of my colleagues were at least a decade my senior, while some were even older than my parents. Although I was with my family, I was plagued by a gnawing feeling that never went away. For a soldier, watching others deploy is like having a rat in your stomach. No matter how much you feed the fucker, it's always hungry. I lasted 16 months before I caved in and disappeared into Iraq.

In a lifestyle that many would consider to be selfish and narcissistic, I met some of the most selfless men I had ever known. Some men delayed their leave by three months or volunteered for the most dangerous tasks not because they had a death wish, but because they wanted to be there to support their mates if things went wrong.

I spent 30 months running operations all over Iraq and Afghanistan, deploying hundreds of consultants on thousands of road moves as part of the reconstruction effort. I was proud that, during that time, we did not suffer or inflict one single casualty. Because I felt uneasy deploying the guys I led most of the road moves. I'm sure my wife – and my mother – would have questioned this decision, but I was genuinely torn between being a proactive husband and father, and supporting my mates who were in harm's way.

In time, I made the decision to leave and return permanently to my family so I could get to know my children. I thought that leaving my action-filled lifestyle would be relatively easy. I was wrong. The transition – like two cars colliding – was chaos. My first day as a home dad was a disaster.

'Where are the nappies?' I asked Colleen as she hurried out the door to work.

'You'll work it out,' she replied, blowing me a kiss. A large smile was plastered across her face. Our three children, Tahlie, Sian and Reyne – aged six, four and two – must have thought: *Who's this pretender? He has no idea.*

My first goal was to get Tahlie to school on time. 'Tahlie, what would you like in your lunch?'

'I don't know,' she replied.

Where is there to go from there? At first I was nice, thinking up half a dozen options. But Tahlie remained undecided. After 10 very frustrating minutes, I made a decision and smothered her sandwich with Vegemite. The result – tears.

'I don't like Vegemite,' she cried.

'Then what *would* you like?' I asked.

'Nutella.'

I threw the Vegemite sandwich in the bin and made one with Nutella. I thought this resolved the whole issue, but as it turned out I had cut the sandwich into squares rather than triangles. More tears, another wasted sandwich, and then it was time to do the girls' hair.

'I want piggies,' said Sian.

'Me too,' said Tahlie.

I gave it a go but no matter how hard I tried, one pigtail always seemed to look twice the size of the other. I settled on ponytails instead and accepted the obvious – more tears. I then heard the radio say it was 10 minutes to nine.

'Quick, kids, brush your teeth, we've got to go,' I yelled.

I bundled Reyne and Sian into the sports pram. We had four minutes to get to school. It was going to be close but I was confident we could make it.

'Dad, Reyne's done a poo in his nappy,' said Tahlie.

'Oh well, he'll just have to sit in it for now — we're not going to be late for school.'

'But it's coming out the sides.'

I peered into the pram and was mortified. *How could such a small child make such a vile mess?* I thought. There was shit everywhere.

I yelled at the kids to come back inside as I quickly put Reyne into the bath. With this complete, and much to Tahlie's disapproval, I squashed all three kids into the pram and, like a man possessed, ran down the hill, the kids hanging on for their lives.

We arrived several minutes after the bell. I didn't bother going to the office to fill out a late note. I preferred denial and definitely didn't need a piece of paper telling me I had screwed up.

We arrived home to a ringing telephone. *I bet it's Colleen checking up on me*, I thought. *Doesn't she know I was in the SAS?*

'Hi, babe, just wanted to let you know that you have mothers' group at 9.30. The kids need the stimulation.'

'Stimulation? I've never been more stimulated in my entire life. I've just spent the last 10 minutes squashing little faecal nuggets down the plug-hole after Reyne defecated in his jumpsuit.'

'Not you, the kids. It's not all about you.'

I threw Sian and Reyne back into the pram and we descended the hill once again, albeit at a much slower pace this time. I didn't mind being late for this one.

That evening, while I was standing at the sink scrubbing burnt chicken from the frypan, Colleen bounced through the door, all smiles.

'How was your day?' she enquired.

I wanted to lie and tell her that it was easy, but all these other words came out: 'I wanted to strangle the little bastards. It was hideous. What did you do to relieve the stress?'

'What do you mean?' she said, laughing.

'I don't know. Do we have anything to drink?'

'Like what?'

'Methylated spirits . . . Something strong to numb my brain,' I spluttered.

After a couple of weeks, I stopped burning the chicken and enrolled at uni. At the end of my first semester, I began to write. I was also employed on a four-day performance training camp for the Australian rugby union team, the Wallabies. Besides catching up with a few of my mates from the Regiment, it was rewarding to work with such highly committed and tough athletes. I was particularly impressed by Phil Waugh, the modest warrior. These men were already high-performing so our aim was to further build their sense of teamwork, and to offer guidance on leadership and decision-making under stress. After six months hanging out with my kids, I felt I was more than qualified for that.

The six members of my team had a tremendous esprit de corps and were committed to taking it to another level. On one afternoon, sitting atop a ridgeline in south-eastern Queensland, the guys were encouraged to share something personal with their mates. This was one of the most moving experiences of my life. I was humbled by the Wallabies' honesty and commitment to each other. There was much more to these guys than brawn.

Negotiating an obstacle with George Gregan and Phil Waugh during a training camp in south-east Queensland.

As a member of our local surf club, I found it equally rewarding to challenge young children and help them gain confidence in the ocean. By the following year, a couple of us established a performance program that catered for the kids who were keen to compete. The initial group of half a dozen young people soon grew to more than 30. At times, watching these eight-year-old children take on three- or four-foot waves left me speechless. Some of these kids were fortunate to be rewarded for their commitment with state medals. But a far greater reward was the ability they gained to conquer their fears. For many, the ocean was once intimidating, but this strength will support them for the rest of their lives.

≡

With Reyne, who's ready to receive a baton during a beach relay.

A few months later, a guy I was training several times a week, a mate by the name of Karl, asked if I would be keen to do some motivational or keynote speaking.

'What do you have in mind?' I asked.

'We might start off with a group of 10 people or so. Have a think about it. I'll try to set something up next year if you're keen.'

Considering that next year was a couple of months away, I confidently said: 'Yeah, why not.' A few days later I received a phone call.

'Hey, mate, I've got you a gig.'

Shit! I thought. 'Really?'

'The guest speaker for an awards ceremony has just pulled out and they're after a replacement.'

'When's it on?' I asked.

'Next week. Can you talk about logistics?'

'Logistics?' I repeated, feeling slightly rattled.

'Yeah, logistics. You'll be addressing 150 people.'

So much for starting off nice and easy. I wanted to say no, but I had a problem: I had recently run a session for Karl that was framed around mental strength.

'Hey, mate,' I'd told him, 'we're doing five sprints up that nasty hill.' The road in question was hideously steep and extended for 400 metres. It offered beautiful views but I knew that after two sprints, taking in the scenery would be the last thing on Karl's mind. 'On one of the runs, I'll give you a head start – I want you to beat me to the top. If you fail, then we're heading straight to the pool and you'll swim 25 metres underwater.' This was something Karl was yet to achieve. 'If you puss out and don't make it all the way, I'll give you one more shot. If you fail again, you can find a new training partner. Any dramas?'

'Jesus, I'm nervous already,' he'd said, laughing.

Although he'd given it a good crack, there had been no way I would have allowed Karl to beat me to the top of that hill. The aim was to fatigue him and burn up his nervous energy. Really, I wanted him to overcome the underwater challenge, which he had struggled with. He was a tough man. I enjoyed training with him and I'd known he could do the underwater swim. Not only did he nail it, but he was so pumped that he'd done it a second time for good measure.

But speaking to such a big audience made me think twice. 'Mate, I don't know. Six days doesn't give me a lot of time to square myself away as a keynote speaker. I'll obviously need to write a speech and put a presentation together. Is there a format I need to follow?'

'You just need to link your experiences back to business. I can give you a few tips.'

You bastard! I thought. 'What do you reckon?'

'You can either take your opportunities or you can let them go.' The tone of his voice said something more: *If you turn this down, you're a freaking pussy.*

I accepted the job and vowed to make him vomit on our next training session.

This led to numerous speaking opportunities. I was surprised by how fragmented a lot of companies were, so one of the themes I often addressed was teamwork. There seemed to be so much internal competition – state versus state, branch versus branch. Rather than working together as a team to outperform their real competitors, people were keeping new and innovative ideas to themselves so they would be recognised for outperforming their own workmates. I knew very little about business, but to me this didn't make sense. Rather than rewarding internal conflict, companies ought to develop a sense of team purpose. If members of a company find a better or more efficient way to do something, they should share the knowledge with their mates.

My new life was busy and I was definitely being challenged, but I still craved the excitement and adrenaline of the SAS. I wondered whether this desire for my past life would ever abate. Was soldiering my destiny, or was I some sort of pretender who wanted to be a dad yet wasn't really capable of sticking it out?

≡

Three weeks before Christmas in 2008, I received an offer to deploy on an anti-piracy task in the Gulf of Aden. Colleen was on holidays at the time and my tertiary commitments wouldn't resume until February. *Perfect timing*, I thought. But I was nervous, and it had nothing to do with the threat. I knew I was someone who struggled with moderation. Many soldiers who leave the Regiment return later. I didn't want to be one of them. Had I really accepted my new life or was I living a lie? There was only one way to find out. I sent off my CV and asked for further information.

During 2008, the year of the economic meltdown, there had been over 100 reported pirate attacks in the waters surrounding Yemen, Oman and Somalia. The hijacking of the Saudi Arabian oil tanker, the MV *Sirius Star*, on its way to the United States with two million barrels of oil was one of the more daring and successful raids of 2008. For Somali pirates, business was booming. In order to safeguard their crews, vessels and cargo, scores of merchant shipping companies sought maritime security.

After receiving further details, I asked Colleen what she thought about it.

'Is it dangerous?'

'Nah . . . It'll be like a cruise, except we get to carry weapons,' I said.

'You're full of it,' she replied, smiling. 'Why do you want to do it?'

'Mick's going . . . It will be great to catch up. And I think there are 15 ex-Regiment guys on the task. It will be a mini SAS reunion.'

'Is that it?'

Negotiations are always fun, I thought. 'It's somewhere different, a new adventure . . . I'm feeling a little restless and I'll get to earn some cash so I can stop bludging off you,' I laughed. 'Seriously, though, it's been almost two and a half years. I want to prove to myself that I'm over going away.' I felt like a little kid begging to go to the shop to buy some lollies.

'How long's it for?'

'Seventeen days, max. I'll be back before Christmas.'

Colleen agreed, I said yes to the offer, and I left for Singapore without even confirming the pay and conditions. The alcoholic licked his lips. I had promised Colleen and the kids that I'd be home before Christmas. This was a test – to see if I could drink in moderation.

≡

I arrived in Singapore on the evening of 6 December 2008 and caught a cab to the hotel. I love the aroma of tropical rain. The air's so thick you can taste it. I got out of the cab and sucked in a couple of deep breaths. I felt alive.

'Good evening, Mr Fennell,' said the receptionist. 'You're sharing a room with Mr Wynne. He has already arrived.'

I was stoked. I probably hadn't seen Wynnie for seven years. I first met him in the Battalion before we both joined the Regiment. We got along well.

I opened the door to my room and saw a massive set of feet hanging over the edge of the bed. They definitely belonged to Wynnie. He's a big man – six-foot-three and 108 kilograms. Not many guys of Wynnie's size pass the selection course, as they usually struggle with endurance. Wynnie was different. He could run, swim and stomp as well as anyone. But the gym was his domain, and when he threw on a set of gloves, the punching bags got nervous.

Wynnie is the perfect guy to share a room with. There's always a steady stream of food flowing through the door, the conversation is interesting and he loves to sleep. I thought Kane was strong in this area, but Wynnie makes Kane look like he's a dieting insomniac. Those two worked together in Bali, running resort security during the high season. I'm sure they came home well rested.

Wynnie is also a deeply reflective and philosophical man. He isn't a fan of city life and prefers the tranquillity of the country, where he lives with his wife. When Wynnie talks about his property – the stream that never runs dry, the old-growth trees that reach upwards forever and the native wildlife that abounds – his large shoulders relax and his face softens. It is his sanctuary.

The next morning I caught up with several of the boys for breakfast. The main reason I accepted the task was to see the guys. For that alone, it was worth it. There were no pauses in the conversation. After breakfast we were taken to the operations room and briefed on the task.

The company's director, a dynamic ex-Regiment soldier who loves to surf, asked what we knew about the task. The answer was: not much.

'Good,' he said, before telling us that we'd be sailing into the Red Sea, where we would rendezvous with several vessels. An armed security team would then be assigned to each vessel before they would move through the Gulf of Aden to Oman, our final destination. It sounded a simple mission, but there were many moving parts. We were all keen to get going.

Wynnie and I, together with a large switched-on Kiwi named Sonny, were sent to Yemen for a meeting with a contact to secure weapons. I initially thought the travel advisory for Yemen was a little ridiculous, giving the impression that any Westerners entering the country would immediately be whisked away by terrorists and never seen again. I had never been to Yemen and was excited to see the place.

But the 2009 slaying and mutilation of a group of aid workers – a British man and his South Korean wife, two German nurses, a German doctor, his wife and three children – reinforced that the threat to Westerners in Yemen was very real.

The airport at Sana'a reminded me of Kabul: primitive, chaotic and tense. We purchased visas, were stamped into the country and exited the terminal. We were unarmed so had to rely on our situational awareness to identify any threats.

'Guys, we'll grab a taxi to the Sheraton,' I said.

We had already discussed what we would do if a vehicle with armed men forced us off the road and attempted to take us hostage. We would simply smile, wave and calmly walk away. If things became hostile we would all break together in the opposite direction – one in, all in. If we became separated we would meet at a designated

In Sana'a, Yemen, with Wynnie.

rendezvous point. If they started shooting, then they would have done it anyway, we thought. Copping a bullet in the back of the head would be more pleasant than having your head hacked off.

We remained alert. Those who hesitate or fail to react allow others to decide their fate. We were in charge of our lives and were determined to keep it that way. It felt good to be operating again.

We found a driver rather than letting one find us. His car wasn't a taxi – there was no meter or distinctive markings. In broken English, our driver told us there were two decent hotels in Sana'a. The Sheraton was, apparently, number two. Our driver, aged in his mid-fifties, wore glasses and carried a large traditional knife on his chest. We soon learned he had a family. He appeared genuine and I tried to keep him talking so we could assess him. I asked him to tell us where the hotel was – how far and in what direction. If he became tense, began driving erratically, in a different direction or tried to make a phone call, we would increase our vigilance. While I questioned him, Wynnie and Sonny searched for additional triggers, such as suspect vehicles trailing us. These observational skills were engrained in us from years of close-quarter battle (CQB), close personal protection (CPP), surveillance and counter-surveillance training.

We checked in to the Sheraton, completed a visual security assessment of the hotel and nominated emergency rendezvous points – both internal and external. It was a large hotel with many rooms. If we were inside and there was a bomb blast or sounds of rifle fire, we would move to a pre-designated room on the fifth floor. Once we had all been accounted for, we would barricade the alcove leading to the door with pieces of heavy furniture, then establish communications with our operations people and wait it out. There was a large military presence in Sana'a. If there was an incident, soldiers would be at the hotel within minutes. Without weapons, our aim was to remain concealed and out of the way – curiosity can be a killer.

If the hotel caught fire and we were threatened, we would make a rope out of the curtains, sheets and blankets. It wouldn't be long enough to reach the ground, but jumping from the second floor was far more appealing than jumping from the fifth. There was also a large tree five metres from our window. Leaping into that would definitely be a last resort, but if we were forced to get out fast, we'd have to take it.

Except in Iraq, Afghanistan, parts of Africa or in international waters, security consultants are rarely armed.

Former SAS soldiers are often employed to complete security surveys and provide close personal protection for VIPs because of their ability to identify threats and implement effective security procedures. If there's a bomb blast, security consultants with the SAS skill-set won't just run with everyone else in the opposite direction, as they are aware that the exits could be channelling people towards a secondary device. The bombing of the Sari Club in Bali was a tragic example of how devastating a secondary explosion can be.

An SAS soldier who has been in the Regiment for six years would have cycled through the counter-terrorism squadron twice and spent at least 24 months 'online'. During this time, he would have made tens of thousands of high-stress decisions, from target recognition and identifying booby traps to assessing doorways and how to react during a single- or double-weapon stoppage. To further develop their skills, it is common for several SAS soldiers to act as the enemy, especially during 'handover training', where one squadron is passing responsibility to another.

In a bomb blast, the first reaction of someone who is well trained will be to assess the situation rapidly, scanning for secondary threats or anything unusual: a truck laden with gas cylinders parked on the sidewalk, a fruit cart with no one selling fruit, an unsecure bicycle with a basket, or even a person acting differently from those around them will stand out to the trained eye. One must think like a terrorist. *If I was going to plant a secondary device, where would it wreak the most carnage?*

≡

Once we had settled into the hotel, I arranged for us to meet a contact in the early afternoon to discuss purchasing weapons. The meeting went well, so I asked to inspect the weapons. Our contact appeared a little reluctant but agreed. We travelled through the city to an affluent neighbourhood. A large set of gates opened, granting us access to a private villa.

Our contact was clearly a busy man – his phone was running hot. We waited in his lounge room while he answered a call. The furniture was basic and practical. There were no decorations or ornaments, just a lounge, television, table and chairs. It was the residence of someone who was busy, someone who didn't have the time or inclination to add warmth or style. The place lacked emotion – it was a bachelor pad that was set up for business.

'Are you ready to see the weapons?' our contact asked after finishing his call.

'Let's do it,' I replied.

We walked into a large room and saw a couple of black pistol cases sitting on a table.

'May we check the weapons?' I asked.

'Of course,' he replied.

The pistol I picked up was a 9-mm Taurus. They were old but well oiled and clean; the slides moved freely. As secondary weapons they would be fine. Leaning against the wall were four AKS-47 assault rifles. Anyone with comprehensive weapons training would never store weapons that way. We cocked the rifles and fired the actions. They weren't ideal, but if our contact couldn't source AK-47s then these would have to do.

'Do you have access to normal AK-47s?' I asked.

'What do you mean normal?'

'These weapons have short barrels, which are good for fighting in confined spaces but they are only accurate to about 100 metres. We'd prefer normal AKs, which have a longer barrel and triple the maximum effective range.'

He wasn't a weapons guy but he understood our concerns. 'Yes, I can get anything.'

He agreed to source AK-47s, but it was no surprise when his guys turned up with more AK-shorts. He also offered to source two RPKs, a long-barrelled derivative of the AK-47 with a bipod, and a couple of 100-round drum magazines, but these didn't eventuate either. Instead he delivered two PKM medium machine guns. Only one of these weapons was serviceable – the second was filthy and corroded. The boys gave them a decent clean and got them singing.

A few days later we had coffee with a large Somali man in Djibouti, northern Africa. He had strong pirate connections and said he was able to source weapons and vessels for our subsequent tasks, but he wanted me to travel with him to Bombasso in Somalia to speak with his contacts as a sign of trust. I was fine with this, as he was business-oriented and appeared to be a man of integrity. He also told us that we wouldn't have any problems with Somali pirates over the next

Sourcing weapons in Sana'a, Yemen.

two weeks – apparently, they would be on holidays. As ridiculous as this sounded, there were religious celebrations taking place.

On the evening of 15 December 2008, 18 of us set sail for the Red Sea in a dodgy dhow. I didn't take any sea-sickness tablets as the Gulf of Aden was like a lake. This, however, would soon change.

At the rendezvous, Tony, Mick and I were allocated to the second vessel, a new tugboat bound for Kuwait. We were all former SAS water operators and had been in the same team – the lead water counter-terrorism assault team – and Tony had commanded it from 2000 to 2002. We had spent many months living in each other's pockets during numerous operational and training deployments. It was refreshing to be hanging out again.

Like me, both Tony and Mick had struggled with their departure from the Regiment. Mick spent over a year in Iraq, and not even a near–death encounter with a roadside bomb could persuade him to give the lifestyle away. But with the breakdown of his marriage, Mick's priorities had

Our dhow in the Red Sea.

changed. Over the next 18 months he dedicated his life to his two young sons, Hunter and Carden. They were his cure and are now his everything.

Tony had been assigned to a training role just prior to the first SAS deployments to Afghanistan. When injury also kept him out of the later deployments, he snapped and got out. Tony stopped socialising with mates who were still in the Regiment. Listening to their experiences had become excruciating, so much so that even attending one mate's funeral was impossible. Tony was not alone in this – there were many others with identical feelings. I was one of them.

Tony is an intellectual man, often consumed by his thoughts. He was aware that his family, especially his five children, needed him. But he also knew they needed a dad who felt fulfilled and challenged. After two brief deployments to the Gulf of Aden, his craving for action settled.

Although there was a significant international naval force patrolling the area, the high-threat zone included some 2.5 million square miles, making it virtually impossible to secure. The Somali pirates were becoming increasingly bold because of their success and the large ransoms they were being paid. They generally operated with the support of a mother craft disguised as a fishing boat. When a target vessel was identified, one or more skiffs – pirate speed boats – would be sent to intercept it. On some of the more complex attacks, they used up to 70 pirates and 20 skiffs.

We weren't permitted to carry weapons aboard our vessel, so we were issued with an LRAD 500 – a non-lethal, directional acoustic hailing device. The hexagonal

LRAD was white and sat atop a tripod. If a rapidly approaching vessel did not heed warnings to change course, the LRAD could be used to send a continuous acoustic tone to deter the attackers. If the vessel closed to within 500 metres, the intensity of the soundwave could be turned up to extremely irritating levels. If a suspect continues to close in, the acoustic tone could reach excruciating levels, to the point where an attacker might receive permanent hearing loss.

Mick and I rehearsed with the LRAD, moving it to numerous locations, to ensure we were able to respond to threats in any direction. While I untied the ropes securing the tripod, Mick disconnected the 240-volt power supply and ran it through the bridge to the opposite side of the vessel. I'd then carry the LRAD to the next location while Mick followed with the tripod. As he reconnected

The LRAD 500, an acoustic hailing device.

the power supply, I donned hearing protection. We rehearsed until we were able to complete the task in less than 30 seconds. With the 20 seconds it took for the device to warm up, this meant we could be operational within 50 seconds.

Tony would remain in the bridge in order to direct the skipper and maintain communications with the flotilla commander, who was located on the lead vessel. Other craft were always positioned to be able to afford mutual support if we were attacked; they had access to automatic weapons, including PKM medium machine guns.

The next morning, we also tested the water cannon and ran rehearsals for the crew. We identified suitable ambush positions where we would be able to disarm the lead attacker with ASP batons. With one of us playing enemy, we adjusted our positions and rehearsed striking an attacker's head as we simultaneously controlled his weapon.

Preparation and planning are instrumental to success. Many years earlier, when I was a junior trooper in the Regiment, Tony had offered me some invaluable advice. I was tasked to run a lesson for the squadron in the lecture theatre. When Tony asked how my rehearsals were going, I said, 'I'm not going to worry about a rehearsal – I know the piece of kit. I'll cuff it.'

His reply: 'Mate, it's easy to tell when someone is cuffing it. If you want to be able to stand up and deliver, then I suggest you do a rehearsal or two. But I'll leave the decision up to you.'

Mick, Tony and I maintained a 24/7 security piquet and increased our vigilance during high-threat times of dusk and dawn. At 0621 on 17 December, a suspect boat was

Observing a suspect vessel in the Gulf of Aden.

identified off our vessel's port side. We readied the LRAD and were operational within 25 seconds. We remained alert until the threat subsided.

By 19 December, the seas had turned angry, battering our convoy with a relentless easterly swell. *So much for the Gulf being like a lake*, I thought. The sea-state, just like the tomatoes I had for breakfast, was on the rise. I could taste the brine in my mouth. *Damn it!* I thought. I knew I had passed the point of no return. I struggled down the stairs and just managed to get my head over the side when the violent contractions commenced. After clearing my stomach, I looked up at the bridge to see if anyone noticed. Mick was standing there laughing. But when the seas reached sea-state six, it was his turn.

The crew, concerned that we had lost our appetites, pressed us to eat. There was no chance – just walking past the galley made me want to throw up.

'*Saya tidak mau makan, aduh, sakit perut*,' I said with absolute conviction, telling them I didn't want to eat because I had a sick stomach. They expressed their sympathy by laughing.

After completing my shift, I went to the bathroom to brush my teeth. *Surely that will make me feel better*, I thought. As the vessel pitched and rolled, I held onto the basin to prevent being thrown about. The air-conditioning wasn't working so the bathroom was hot and stuffy. But it was the dreadful stench that wafted from the toilet that pushed me over the edge. I flicked off the lid of my toothpaste, held the tube close to my nostrils and sniffed like a coke addict. This only accentuated my desire to vomit. It was pathetic and I laughed in between contractions.

The following morning we learned that several guys on the other vessels had been vomiting. When I was asked how we were going, I decided to be up-front and honest. 'No dramas here,' I replied. But the next 36 hours were torturous. We were aboard a tugboat that was designed to operate in harbours. A sea-state six made things rather uncomfortable.

The following day we closed in on the coast of Oman. Late that afternoon, we observed two vessels moving across our front. We slowed down to assess the situation and readied the LRAD. The conditions were atrocious. The boats were heading towards Oman, possibly trying to escape the weather. We continued on.

At last we reached our destination, the port of Salalah. The hotel we checked in to was filthy – my bed looked like someone had been sleeping in it. The next day I flew home, arriving on the morning of 23 December. I had only spent 17 days away – almost nothing in comparison to years past – yet it was definitely long enough. I really missed taking the kids down to the beach.

≡

I knew my transition was complete when I had the opportunity to deploy at short notice to Afghanistan with the reserve Commandos over Christmas. It wouldn't be the same as going with the Regiment, but it was still an operational deployment. There were several reasons why I wanted to go, the strongest being to deploy with Al, one of my closest brothers. Al and I have been mates since primary school.

When Al had asked me to be his best man, he handed me a bottle of beer. The brand read:

Alexander
Keith's

'Why's your name first?' I asked, grinning.

'Yeah, but your name's written in larger letters.'

'That's true. Cheers, big guy.'

Al is a part-time Commando and is also studying medicine. For someone with a ridiculously high IQ, he's pretty funny, coordinated and surprisingly normal.

Al had his reasons for wanting to deploy, and although he asked for my opinion, he knew his decision had to come from within. As for me, after much deliberation I turned the opportunity down. I didn't want to spend another four months away from my family, especially over Christmas. Unless my circumstances changed, I would only contemplate short tasks. I had spent more than a decade going away; now that I knew what it was like to be a dad, I wasn't prepared to give that up. Perhaps people do change.

The week before Al left, I threw him off a 45-metre bridge into the ocean. He was attached to a rope. The abseil was spectacular. We also went for a fast run.

Al serving in Afghanistan.

'I'm going to set a cracking pace, mate,' I told him. 'This is similar to the speed an SAS troop runs when they're going hard. I want you to beat me to the other end of the bridge.'

He did. It was obvious Al had trained hard. Physically and mentally, he was ready to go to war.

Since Al's deployment, two Australian soldiers have been killed in Afghanistan. I heard about the first incident on the news, and I immediately thought of him. Al wasn't just a mate, he was a brother. A day later I found a message on my mobile from a voice I didn't recognise. I listened to it at least five times, then played it to Colleen.

'Who do you reckon this is?' I asked her.

'Don't know. I've never heard the voice before,' she replied.

I played the message again. 'Do you think it could be Al?'

'Nah, it's definitely not Al.'

I listened again, trying to connect some part of the

message to the guy I had known since I was five. 'You're right. It's not him,' I said.

But it had been Al. He'd been out on patrol when a soldier 15 metres in front of him tripped an improvised explosive device and disappeared. For this man, death was instantaneous, but for his family his death lingers forever. You can try to justify a death like this to those who are grieving, but in the end, when someone you love dies, it's just fucking sad.

Al's voice had carried the tone of a much older man. It was a lifeless voice – serious, distant and vague. We spoke later that day.

'You alright, mate?' I asked.

'Yeah, I'm fine. It's sad – he was a good guy.'

'I was hoping it was you so I could have your motorbike,' I said with a laugh.

Al laughed too. 'Yeah, well, you'll have to wait.'

Phone calls from soldiers on deployment are always guarded and a little weird, as they can't speak freely. I never asked Al what he'd been up to and he didn't discuss anything operational. I knew what it was like, so I spent the time telling him that he was missing out on a great summer.

Two weeks later a 107-mm rocket passed within 40 centimetres of Al's head. One of his mates wasn't so lucky. Although they had been struck by a violent hand, the Commandos' commitment to each other only intensified. For years Al had heard my stories; now it felt strange to be on the receiving end. But I was proud of him. Not a condescending, big-brother proudness. He was a mate and a soldier who had handled himself well under testing conditions.

I'm not sure how Al will find the transition from war to civilian life. The sounds, smells and images of war will remain etched in his long-term memory, but so too will the camaraderie that was forged during adversity.

One day we'll chat about it.

EPILOGUE

History provides a rich collection of stories of soldiers and armies who have displayed something special – those who have blended brains, courage and brawn. When I read about the Battle of Thermopylae, I was so impressed by the commitment and loyalty of King Leonidas' men to each other that I used their actions for motivation when working with the Auckland Warriors rugby league side in the lead-up to the team's 2008 NRL finals campaign.

The Auckland Warriors were an impressive outfit of men who displayed a wonderful combination of the warrior's spirit and humility. For me, it was an honour to have been invited to work with such a fine group of men. Their sense of teamwork and mateship was on par with that of my brothers in the Regiment, and like many SAS soldiers, they were heavily inked with meaningful tattoos.

Ahead of the team's vital match against the Melbourne Storm on 14 September 2008, I sent an email to their conditioning coach, Craig Walker, who pinned my message on the boys' lockers:

In 480 BC, King Leonidas of Sparta led 300 Spartans and 2000 Thespians and other Greek allies against a Persian army of 80,000 men. King Leonidas was offered control of Greece if he surrendered. His answer was, 'If you had any knowledge of noble things in life, you would refrain from coveting others' possessions; but for me to die for Greece is better than to be the sole ruler over the people of my race.' He was then asked to surrender his arms, to which he replied, 'Come and get them.'

During the first Persian assault, the Spartans cut their adversaries to pieces. Over the next two days, 10,000 Persians attacked the Spartans and failed. Another 50,000 Persians joined the battle. They also failed. The 300 Spartans were eventually defeated, but not before they destroyed 20,000 of their enemy.

All you have to do is defeat 13 other men. It doesn't sound that difficult when you think about what some other warriors have achieved throughout history.

Men are made up of blood, bone, meat and brain. Nothing more! No man or team is invincible. Take their measure and then take some more.

In the history of the NRL, no team in eighth position had defeated the minor premiers in the first round of finals. The Auckland Warriors, just like the Spartans, fought as a team and punched well above their weight. The Warriors were victorious while the Spartans eventually lost their lives, but both had self-belief and were not intimidated by the strength of their opponents.

Giving advice to others is one thing, but I also realise the value of self-criticism. I regularly reflect on my own shortfalls. Unless you're aware of your weaknesses, how can you possibly become stronger?

I have been addicted to adrenaline and the rush associated with working in dangerous locations. The time when you're fighting for survival is also the time when you feel most alive. It is near-on impossible to recapture this feeling in regular life. Trust me – I have nearly drowned trying.

When soldiers return from war, especially if they have had near-death experiences, they sometimes develop an attitude of invincibility – a bit like adolescent males who are charged with testosterone. Having been there, I know the feeling. I'm also aware that this mindset can be more perilous than bullets or bombs. Your ability to acknowledge danger can be more relaxed than that of someone who hasn't experienced such things. What others consider to be dangerous, returned soldiers sometimes view as acceptable, or even as desirable.

I have done some crazy shit in my time, including leaping off a bridge into water in the middle of the night without assessing the risk. After having a large quantity of salt water forced into my arse at high-speed and bruising my tailbone, culminating with six weeks of discomfort, I realised that there is a fine line between seeking adventure and making bad decisions.

Although I like to challenge myself in the ocean, especially when it gets a little nasty out there, I work hard on my fitness and skills, which gives me the ability to extend myself. My training includes underwater work, a combination of both high- and low-heart-rate breath holds.

I was recently stuck in the impact area of a large surf after losing my board. For over 15 minutes I was repeatedly sucked to the bottom and held under for 10 to 20 seconds at a time. The water was so aerated that I was unable to swim to the surface. Every time I needed a breath, I had to dive to the bottom and launch off the sand. I was rarely able to steal more than one breath before being sucked through the next wave and driven back down. I was telling myself to calm down and relax – drowning on my local beach would be bloody embarrassing. The three large blue-bottles that were wrapped around my neck were the least of my concerns – I'm sure they hated the experience as much as me. I eventually made it in, 350 metres down the beach. When I got to the car I noticed my lips were blue; I was hypoxic.

I'd be a liar if I said the experience didn't rattle me a little. The next day I jumped in the pool with a couple of mates and did some underwater work. Training and preparation are critical for anyone who likes to push the limits.

Sadly, a young male exchange student from Saudi Arabia also ventured into the surf that night; he had been celebrating his 25th birthday with a group of friends. It was late, he was a poor swimmer, the surf was treacherous and he had been drinking. I knew how difficult I had found the conditions – the poor guy didn't stand a chance.

For people like me, my mates, young adolescent males and soldiers who are trying to negotiate their way back to a more banal lifestyle, I try to remember this: if we must fall, then let it be the hand of fate, not waste, or while doing what we love; our fleeting moments of madness should not remain forever.

≡

Over the last couple of years I have heard of soldiers from several countries who boast about taking life, as if the experience should give them special status or joy. For me, such comments either show a false bravado or belie far deeper problems: that they have been desensitised to the point that they are out of touch with society. Killing may be integral to war, but it is not a sport. In war, there are no trophies and there are no winners.

Some guys pretend they are winners – a false ideal that is usually accentuated when in the presence of others and alcohol. But I challenge these men to rise from their beds in the middle of the night, walk to the bathroom, face the mirror and peer deep into the eyes before them. When there is no one to challenge their ego, when the night is as quiet as a corpse, what sort of man do they see? When they close their eyes and picture the faces and bodies of those who breathe no longer, do these indelible images give them the same uplifting feelings as watching children play?

For me, catching a wave, having a laugh with a few mates or hanging out down at the beach with my family gives me joy. And like any parent, I'm definitely guilty when it comes to bragging about the exploits of my children. Taking life does not define who I am: it is something I have had to do and it brings me neither guilt, pride nor joy. It was a requirement of war, and the memory of it gives me a hollow, dead feeling that I don't like to think about.

In the lead up to Anzac Day this year, I spoke with a number of World War II veterans who, to this day, still harbour a deep hatred for those who they met in battle. But these men were usually subjected to horrors that we may not fully understand. Despite this hatred, I have never heard one of these vets speak of taking life as if they had just hit the cricket ball over the fence for six. That is one thing I love about the elderly: they are more inclined to tell it how it is, rather than try to be perceived as something they are not.

Throughout my life I have gained inspiration, knowledge and guidance from many people, from family and friends to martial arts instructors and SAS patrol commanders. I have also drawn strength from people I barely know. Whenever I meet someone special, I try to ascertain what it is that makes them unique. It could be the way they have dealt with adversity, or how they have reached the top of their chosen field, or how their actions have had a positive effect on the lives of others. I find myself analysing them and hoping that a small piece of them will rub off on me.

But I don't gauge my success by comparing myself to others. Those who do so are often left bitter and fail to reach their potential. I compete with myself, because then the potential for growth is infinite; I am not bordered by those above and below.

My experiences, training and relationships have shaped my life, but the way I reflect on these things allows me to grow and progress with confidence. Not everything I attempt works out, but I give everything I attempt the same level of commitment.

Acknowledgements

*Those who have had the greatest impact upon my life
are those who have been the most generous with their time.
Sincere thanks.*

*I would also like to thank my editor, Julian Welch, for his vision,
efficiency and attention to detail. You're a legend, mate!*

In memory of our warrior brother, Danny G

1969–2009